A PLACE IN
GOD'S HEART

OTHER BOOKS BY
KAY D. RIZZO

Adventist Girl, set two
For His Honor
I Will Die Free
The Secret Dreams of Dolly Spencer

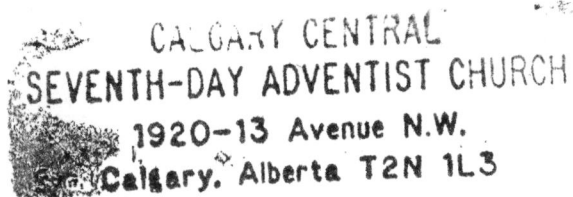

A PLACE IN GOD'S HEART

*Finding joy
in His presence*

KAY D. RIZZO

PACIFIC PRESS® PUBLISHING ASSOCIATION
Nampa, Idaho
Oshawa, Ontario, Canada
www.PacificPress.com

Designed by Michelle C. Petz
Cover photo copyright © Philip Porcella / Getty Images

Copyright © 2003 by
Pacific Press® Publishing Association
Printed in the United States of America
All Rights Reserved

Additional copies of this book are available by calling toll free 1-800-765-6955 or visiting
http://www.adventistbookcenter.com.

Library of Congress Cataloging-in-Publication Data

Rizzo, Kay D., 1943-
A place in God's heart : finding joy in His presence / Kay D. Rizzo.
p. cm.
ISBN: 0-8163-2011-X
1. Christian life—Seventh-day Adventist authors. I. Title.

BV4501.3.R59 2oo4
248.4'86732—dc22   2003066420

03 04 05 06 07 • 5 4 3 2 1

DEDICATION

*To Richard, my friend,
my confidante, and my soul mate.*

CONTENTS

INTRODUCTION

Jesus said, "Whatever is in your heart determines what you say"
(Luke 6:45, NLT).

Everywhere I go, I hear or I read about the remarkable power of the Internet. On line, I can shop for Christmas gifts from Pitcairn Island, have my "disease de jour" diagnosed by a doctor in Donegal, or argue Iraqi politics with a computer nerd in Nairobi. And it's all done with words.

Stocks are traded. Fortunes rise and fall. Words determine the fate of Caesars, Czars, and U.S. Congressmen. Every military campaign ever mapped out, every battle fought, every victory won, began with words.

John called Jesus "the Word." The heavens were made by the Word of God—Jesus Christ. Divine power through Jesus' words straightened deformed limbs, reconstructed eyes in empty sockets, rebuilt noses devoured by leprosy, and flung demons into swine. Jesus' words silenced storms, raised the dead, and healed wounded and abused hearts. Simple words combined with divine impact!

Christ's life and words demonstrated His powerful love for you and me. The Savior would rather die than live forever in a perfect environment without us. The ultimate evidence of that love was found in the unbelievable words He uttered on Calvary: "Father, forgive them."

As the demons of hell were preparing for their victory dance, Jesus Christ did the unexpected, the unthinkable. He forgave. When the world expected curses, He gave them forgiveness.

Today, the Savior's words contain that same power to straighten, to heal, and to reconstruct malformed lives. When I choose to fill my heart with Jesus' love, my words and actions will reflect that love.

Living the words of Jesus is the adventure of a lifetime. Think about it. You and I can live in the continual essence of divine presence through His words. Can you imagine living each and every day, each and every hour, each and every minute, each and every second, bubbling over with life, love, joy, peace, patience, and tenderness? You can, you know. I can too. The Savior gave us the keys to the abundant life. We need only to use them.

Did you know that you *already* have a place in God's heart? Discover how to live the abundant life by finding joy in His presence.

LIVING THE MORE ABUNDANT LIFE

I am come that they might have life,
and that they might have it more abundantly
(John 10:10, KJV).

Living beautifully and loving it? That's me! Jesus is describing my life!

Where do I live? Surely not planet Earth! Living beautifully in a world of graft, greed, and government betrayal—is it an anomaly or an out-and-out lie? How can I laugh and sing amidst a daily deluge of disease, death, and deception? Can joy bubble up from my inmost soul while living in a place where deranged mothers drown their babies in bathtubs and angry men gun down their wives and children and then turn the gun on themselves? Is it realistic to think I can live a beautiful life in this nasty, nitty-gritty world of the twenty-first century?

Jesus Christ said, "I am come that you might have life and have it more abundantly." Surely He foresaw the terror and mayhem of this era. Yet He said, "I've come that you might live an abundant life." Abundant life? Do you find it incredible to imagine that such a state is possible in a world in which eight-year-olds sexually attack, maim, and kill three-year-old siblings for the sport of it? Can an abundant life be possible in a world in which grieving parents watch as the lifeless bodies of their loved ones are extricated from bombed-out pizza parlors and shopping malls? How can joy be mine seeing teenagers blow themselves up with homemade bombs for senseless causes?

Hey, that's the reality of my world; that's the reality of yours. Does the Master's offer of abundant life apply to this mess?

In the first century A.D., the apostle Peter didn't face a two-hour commute to the office. Dr. Luke didn't patch up victims of a 100-car pileup on a foggy interstate or extricate mangled bodies from a derailed train. Wealthy Lydia didn't have to fear flying in a jet commandeered by a terrorist from a "faraway place with a name lifted from the Dead Sea Scrolls." These faithful individuals of the first century faced none of the high-tech terrors that create trauma for today's women, men, and children. No wonder they were filled with abundant joy!

I realize that their daily lives weren't lifted from Eve's Garden of Eden prayer journal either, but they had to be more relaxed and serene than ours. A hymn writer of another era wrote about traveling with Jesus, traversing "the little hills of Galilee," where "a sweet peace fills the air." A stubbed toe or two, a scratch from a thorn bush—hardly the material for reporting on the evening news. Even a skirmish or two with a Roman guard, a mugging on the road to Jericho, or an uprising among the Zealots sounds mild compared with CNN's top story of the hour—at any hour, of any day or night.

I confess I wear rose-tinted contact lenses when regarding the past. For me, time casts a romantic haze over bygone eras. For instance, who knew how great life was in the 1960s until we relived it from vantage point of 2004? Or who would have imagined the attraction today's youth would find in the '50s sack dress, French twist, and Audrey Hepburn's neck? Even Elvis Presley's "Jail House Rock" doesn't seem so evil measured against the gangster rap of today.

Another glamorized era is that of the American westward migration. We eulogize the tales of pioneers crossing deserts, mountains, and prairie—forgetting that they traveled without the benefits of air-conditioned SUVs, Golden Arches eateries, and a Marriot Hotel's indoor pool and Jacuzzi™ in which to unwind at the end of the day. The sepia hues of time soften the edges of the travelers' discontent.

It is difficult to imagine doing without hot showers and indoor plumbing or cooking without a microwave oven. My mind glosses over the reality of persistent gnats and pesky flies buzzing around my face; the ache in my shoulders and back; the sting of blisters on my feet as I trudge west from Missouri or Nebraska.

My imagination conveniently obliterates the poisonous snakes under the sagebrush or the pungent odors of my fellow travelers who haven't bathed in more than a month! I am deaf to the griping inevitably associated with selfish, tired, and discontent human beings—by far the most lethal and volatile element of the journey. And threats of Indian attack, tornados, flash floods, or prairie fires merely add romance to my adventure—certainly not any real discomfort or danger.

As a child I listened to tales of my ancestors' voyage from "jolly, olde England" to Virginia's wild, unsettled shores. Proudly I claimed the heroes of my heritage—the Hancocks, the Sherwoods, the Madisons, the Ryans, and the Balls—God-fearing colonists all. The word *abundant* certainly describes their vision and their adventures as they transplanted European civilization to the North American continent. They lived the lavish promise of John 10:10.

Yesterday—the Colonial Era, the westward migration, even the 1950s—is gone forever. As my teenage friends would say, "Get over it." Today and tomorrow are what is important to my life. So what about me, what about you? What does living an abundant life have to do with the raw reality of our lives in the nasty here and now?

The word *abundant* means "plentiful, ample, more than enough." Scriptural examples of abundance include the twelve baskets of leftovers after Jesus fed the five thousand from one little boy's lunch. The wedding story where Jesus turned water into wine is another example of God's supplying an abundance. Imagine the servants filling six, twenty- to thirty-gallon jugs with water. Christ's miracle would produce between 120 and 180 gallons of wine, a super-abundant amount of refreshment for any party.

God's abundance is evident throughout creation. He is the Creator of the infinite! By Sabbath morning of Creation week, planet Earth was teeming with life, exploding with variety. And His creation didn't stop with day seven. Today His creative process continues. He's the Creator—yesterday, today, and forever.

In both the Old and New Testaments, He says, " 'No eye has seen, no ear has heard, no mind has conceived what God has prepared for those who love him' " (1 Corinthians 2:9; see also Isaiah 64:4). If you have a know-no-bounds imagination like mine, wrap your mind around the word picture in my very own Rizzo paraphrase of that verse, "The surprises God has in store for me are more vibrant and exciting than anything my eyes can see; His music surpasses the outer limits of my hearing abilities; and that's just the beginning. His abundance outstrips my wildest flights of fancy."

The Master promised His disciples an abundant life. Was it a real promise or merely a wish? Did Paul experience abundance while confined in his underground prison cell? What about Stephen, as the first stone pummeled his body? Did he sense that his life was beautiful? Consider John penning his missives from a lonely, windswept island. Were his days filled with abundant joy as well?

The Bible answers Yes to all these questions. Jesus Himself promises that I can live a life of abundance. Was He speaking in hyperbole? Was He exaggerating about the possibilities in His promise? I don't think so. I think Jesus meant every word—literally. He wants my life to be a showcase for salvation. He wants me to show off for Him. (Even the tiniest flame shines brightly in a cave.) He wants the world to see that there is something different, something magical, and something bigger-than-life for those who choose to live in His presence.

Look around you while sitting in church next weekend. Do you see joy on the worshipers' faces? Is the abundant life happening in your church, in your neighborhood, in your home, in your life? If not, what did first-century Christians know about living an extravagantly abundant life in Christ that we have somehow missed?

Several years ago I was on the other side of the abundant life that Christ promised. No, I wasn't dead, but at the time, I felt as if and wished I were—enough to contemplate a method and a means. The phrase "abundant life" meant nothing to me. My life was abundant in wheezing and weeping. I couldn't imagine facing another day. When I tried to seek God through His Book, the words blurred before my eyes. When I sought Him in prayer, my mind wouldn't focus. When I reached out to His other children, I was rebuffed. My future was filled with hopelessness. My heart was filled with fury. I wallowed in a murky spiritual pit. I didn't know then that total disillusionment would be a necessary step to my rebirth. It wasn't until much later that I discovered that I needed to become disillusioned with everything I had once believed before I was ready to listen to God.

The Creator of the universe who "heals . . . diseases, . . . redeems . . . life from the pit and crowns . . . with love and compassion" (Psalm 103:3, 4), used the very pain that had drained my body of energy—my anger—to reignite my spirit once more.

He began by drawing my attention to the words of Revelation 3:11— " 'Hold on ... so that no one will take your crown.' " You see, I was angry—angry at the world. My enemies had stolen enough of my life— my health, my livelihood, my self-respect, my joy, and my peace. And they were working on stealing my family. I wasn't about to let them steal my crown as well!

Clutching those words with all the strength I had left, I allowed God to lead me to the "cursing" Psalms. That's right, the cursing Psalms. David had some harsh and fiery things to say against his enemies. And I savored every verse. Somehow I knew that if David was called, "a man after God's own heart," my heavenly Father wouldn't reject me for claiming David's curses as mine.

I relished the flavor of the psalmist's "get-even" phrases. I could vicariously bring down fire and brimstone on my enemies. I could break their teeth (Psalm 58:5-7) and scatter their bones in the dust. While I found little peace in my cries of vengeance, my fevered brain uncovered something more valuable. Even as I generously heaped scriptural curses on my enemies, I discovered that words of praise to God either followed or preceded each curse.

One morning God's message broke through my myopia. I realized that the peace, love, and joy I was seeking weren't found in the psalmist's fury, but in the psalmist's praise. As my diatribes turned to rejoicing, the Creator could then heal my heart—one hurt at a time. He replaced my sorrow, not with a live-for-the-moment pleasure I might find at an amusement park, but with a deeply-rooted-in-the-soul, mind-altering joy. Surprise! Surprise! My heavenly Father didn't change His message; He changed me.

Like a sip of cold spring water on a mid-summer day, this experience awakened a thirst within me for more and more and more. My cravings for this new-found joy led me through the Psalms and into the New Testament, in particular, to Paul's letter to the Philippians. "Rejoice in the Lord always, and again [in case you didn't get the message the first time] I say, Rejoice!" (Philippians 4:4, Rizzo paraphrase).

Here's evidence of the sensational lifestyle Jesus promised His disciples in John 10:10. Here's the joy of which the Savior spoke only minutes prior to His fierce and lonely battle in Gethsemane. But first, He said, there would be pain. "I tell you the truth, you will weep and mourn while the world rejoices. You will grieve, but your grief will turn to joy" (John 16:20).

Pain? I could relate. Grief, I understood. I had experienced devastating losses—the death of two fathers and three children. But when would my grief turn to joy? Could I expect an abundant life of joy, peace, faith, and hope in my life on this side of the heavenly kingdom? Or would I have to wait for His return?

I'd lived long enough to know that an abundant life didn't necessarily include a mansion overlooking San Francisco Bay or a Lincoln Explorer parked in my "carriage house." I knew I would never find Paul's incredible joy at the bottom of a whiskey bottle or in a porno Web site.

I also realized that my family's love, no matter how strong and how constant it had been throughout my spiritual winter, could never completely fill the God-sized, gaping hole in my soul.

As a little child, I'd given my heart to Jesus, so I knew where to turn. Instinctively I knew there had to be more to the abundant life than the asthmatic, inhale-exhale existence I'd been experiencing. There had to be something better. This couldn't be "as good as it gets." And I was determined to find that better life. I would no longer be content to live spiritually with a half-a-loaf mentality; I wanted the entire seven-course, banquet-sized, God-filling feast of joy, peace, love, and hope.

I would no longer be satisfied living like the penniless Irishman who sold all his belongings and scraped together every six pence and pound he could in order to fulfill his life-long dream of immigrating to America. With barely enough money to pay for his passage on the ship, the man used the last few coins in his pocket to buy five, day-old loaves of bread. At each mealtime, he snuck away to his berth to eat his stale dry bread in secret. He had so little; he couldn't afford the luxury of sharing his small cache of food with other hungry passengers.

On the last day of his voyage, a fellow traveler with whom the man had struck up a conversation suggested they continue their conversation over dinner. Embarrassed, the Irishman confessed he lacked the money to eat in the dining room.

"What are you talking about?" his new friend asked. "Where have you been taking your meals?"

His traveling companion gaped in disbelief as the Irishman admitted his dark secret. "But didn't you know that the price of your ticket covered all your meals?"

Paid in full. The poor man, living for a week on stale bread and water when he could have had full meals in the dining room!

My place at God's abundant table was included with the price of my ticket to heaven—the death of Jesus Christ on the cross. Do you know anyone like the hapless Irishman who doesn't believe God's abundant life was meant for him, at least not on this earth, not while plodding over the long, rocky, narrow road to heaven? Too many heirs of

God's kingdom live as if they were part of the homeless poor when they could be luxuriating in their Father's abundance.

Putting a human face on a heavenly concept, can you imagine a queen's son or a president's daughter choosing to suffer in pain-filled silence during a personal crisis? Can you see an offspring of the rich and famous choosing to forego his or her birthright to the family's wealth while traveling in a distant land? With our family vault overflowing with life's greatest and best treasures, should God's kids settle for any less than the best Father God has to offer—a life in the abundance?

Back to our misinformed Irishman and his cache of stale bread. Surely he had seen, smelled, and salivated over the hot food in the dining room. Surely he longed for a taste of ice-cold melon or a bowl of hearty stew.

Have you been craving a more abundant life but have been settling for your secret cache of stale bread? Do you graze in your "spiritual refrigerator" and see nothing to satisfy your nagging midnight hunger? Do you find yourself scrounging around the bottom of life's popcorn bowl for stale "dead heads" of happiness when in your heart you yearn for the "poppingest" of joy? Do you long for a day-by-day peace beyond verbal description but can't believe that such a life is available in today's world? Are you tired of the ho-hum sameness in your worship and you ache to "celebrate God all day, every day ... [to] revel in him"? (Philippians 4:4, *The Message*).

You don't need to be on the verge of starvation to desire something more in your spiritual diet. You don't have to grovel with the family pets for food scraps from God's table. You just need to admit you are hungry—you know, the way my five-year-old grandson does. "Grandma, I'm hungry," is enough to melt my heart.

Jesus said, "You're blessed when you've worked up a good appetite for God. He's food and drink, in the best meal you'll ever eat" (Matthew 5:6, *The Message*). A simple yen for Heaven's delicacies, a tantalizing thirst for Christ's living water is all you really need. And God will grant your wish.

The Father intends for you and me to live above and beyond the ho-hum, day-after-day boredom of falling into and crawling out of sin.

Even the most exciting sin-based pleasures become boring when repeated over and over, and over, and over again. And once you've exhausted all 113 sins as listed in the Word of God, what then?

The opposite is true with God-inspired pleasures. You and I can live in the very essence of His presence. This life that Jesus promised can only get richer, beginning on this earth and continuing for all eternity. The best is yet to come!

At the end of each chapter in this book are exercises that can help you discover and enjoy an abundant life like the one Jesus describes in John 10:10. These daily recipes for joy can add fiber and vitality to your spiritual diet. They can help turn your primetime moments of delight into a daily habit of gratitude and praise. The joy-filled, abundant life Jesus presents to the children of the new millennium can be yours. What do you say? Break out your best silver and linen. We're going to feast on God's abundance.

GRACE NOTES

- Begin a praise journal in which you can record each new concept that will enrich your worship time with God. If you aren't a journalist, record your discoveries in cassette tape to play back later.
- Make a list of the evidences of God's abundance in your life—one blessing per Post-it note. Scatter those notes about your home. Post them where you can read them every day.
- Share a sample of God's abundance in your life with someone else for no reason other than because you can. Suggestion: Make a triple batch of your favorite cookies. Put them in re-closeable plastic bags, add a bow, and give them to kids or retirees in your neighborhood.
- Stir up a new recipe or sauté an exotic vegetable you've never eaten before. While savoring the unfamiliar flavors on your tongue, recite the following scripture: "Taste and see that the Lord is good" (Psalm 34:8).

QUEST FOR CONTENTMENT, SEARCH FOR SATISFACTION

Be content with what you have, because God has said,
"Never will I leave you; never will I forsake you"
(Hebrews 13:5).

At a recent women's retreat, I was rehearsing for special music when my accompanist and long-time friend paused, her fingers lingering on the piano keys.

"Kay, I have a spiritual hunger gnawing inside of me. There has to be something more to life than this. I hear people talk about joy and praise and the abundant life, but I've never experienced it. I've been a Christian all my life; I grew up in a Christian home and have raised my children in a Christian home as well. Yet, sometimes I feel so empty." A sigh conveyed her frustration. "When I try to talk to my husband about it, he clams up. He says I'm never satisfied with what I have. Honestly, I'm not complaining, but I am so starved for life-changing evidence of the Holy Spirit. There just has to be something more."

I knew how my friend felt. I'd been there. For years, like a spiritual tornado, I whipped through church-related activities that were guaranteed to relieve my boredom and stimulate my exhaustion. Yet deep inside I knew, like my friend, there had to be more to this Christian life than what I'd experienced. As a result, I would search harder for ways to become busier. Then, when my spurts of physical energy sputtered and failed, dissatisfaction would settle deeper into my soul. In an effort to find solace in my disappointment, I would repeat Paul's admonition, "Be content with what you have" (Hebrews 13:5).

Contentment and *satisfaction*—are these words interchangeable? The dictionary describes *satisfaction* as "gratification, having your fill of what you expect, need, or desire." *Contentment* means "to gladly accept what is given to you, knowing that more can be yours—being happy with one's lot."

My five-year-old grandson, Jarod, knows the difference between these two concepts. When I take him to the park, he begs me to push him on the swings. "Higher, Grandma! Push me higher!" he cries. When he reaches the height where the chains begin to rattle, he shouts, "Enough, Grandma. That's high enough." He's satisfied!

However, at my table, when I place on his plate a serving of lettuce, tomatoes, and jumbo-sized black olives, freshly blended with Grandpa Rizzo's customized dressing, Jarod is content, knowing "there's more where that came from."

Do you see the difference? The biblical charge to "be content with what you have" doesn't mean to forgo one's desires—the very dreams and goals God implanted in your heart and mind. Jeremiah 29:11 says, " 'I know the plans I have for you,' declares the LORD, 'plans to prosper you and not to harm you, plans to give you hope and a future.' " Settling for less than God's best would thwart God's perfect plan for your life.

In God's Word, *contentment* usually often refers to material possessions. For instance, Hebrews 13:5: "Keep your lives free from the love of money and be content with what you have, because God has said, 'Never will I leave you; never will I forsake you.' " In the original Greek manuscript, the word *never* in this text is used, not once but four times.

"I will never, never, never, never leave you nor forsake you." Repeating the phrase adds emphasis to the word *never*—*never* in the superlative, for all eternity! How emphatic is that?

We can be content with our share of the earth's bounty because God has promised to supply all our needs. That makes sense. There'll never be a time when we need to fear that He might leave us and force us to "go it alone." He'll always be there for us—He promises.

The promise of Psalm 37:25 reads, "I was young and now I am old, yet I have never seen the righteous forsaken or their children begging bread." As a youth I quaked with fear at the idea that, during the "time of the end," God's Spirit would be removed from the earth. How could any of us survive without God's Spirit within us?

Today my arsenal of heavenly warrantees assures me that, while God's Spirit may be removed from the earth at some time, He will never leave His children. His guarantees are certain. God will never, never, never, never abandon me to the wiles of Satan. He will never, never, never, never fail to meet my needs. He will never, never, never, never leave me defenseless against the divinations of the father of lies. He's given His word. God cannot lie. Through tough times or good, I can hold on to that truth. You can too.

Humberto Noble Alexander, a mechanic and lay-preacher, spent twenty-two years as a political prisoner in Cuba for preaching about the second coming of Jesus to the young people in his church. In his book *I Will Die Free,* Pastor Alexander tells of the time his captors made him stand on his tiptoes, chin-deep, in the prison lake-sized cesspool. One hour, two hours, three hours, the muscles in his feet and legs cramped into tight, painful knots.

The sun grew hotter. The stench burned his nostrils and eyes. Feeling abandoned and desperate, he cried out in agony, "Dear God, where are You in all of this?"

God answered the prisoner's question by drawing his attention to a lily pad floating a few feet from his face. As the sun climbed to its apex in the sky and the temperatures grew hotter, Noble watched a small bud begin to open into a pure white, aromatic flower. The beauty and fragrance from that perfect white lily blocked from his consciousness the slime, filth, and decay surrounding him. Where was God during Noble's time of need? Where He'd always been. The perfect Lily of the Valley, the Rose of Sharon was right there with him in the filthiest of life's muck and mire.[1]

After Eden's gates closed behind our first parents, life on planet Earth has never been easy. If you haven't experienced difficult times yet, wait, you will. Pain and disappointment are facts of life on this sin-encrusted orb. Scripture says, "The rain falls on the good and the evil." And yet, in the face of destitution and despair, you and I can cling to the words of the psalmist, "I have never seen the righteous forsaken or their children begging bread."

No matter how rough life became over the years—and the Rizzos have had their share of rocky roads to travel—we have always had food on our table and clothes on our bodies. Just as God traveled with Richard's dad, a lonely teenage boy, from Calabria, Italy, to New York City, just as God maintained a supply of potatoes in my parents' barren pantry during the Great Depression, so He has been a constant companion to Richard and me. While there were times when our clothes came to us courtesy of Goodwill Industries, and more than one evening meal consisted of corn bread and cold milk, we've not merely existed over the years—we've thrived!

And that abundance of divine blessings have continued on into the lives of our children, and should time last, will be evident in the homes of our grandsons. I am confident because He said He would be with us. "Thus saith the Lord." Simple, isn't it? God is worthy of our trust.

Trust—another casualty of our age. Who can you trust? Physicians? Lawyers? Preachers? CPAs? Corporate CEOs? What about the government? Perhaps with all the greed around you, you've decided that you can depend only on yourself.

Have you ever been down to your last $10 bill? Did you squirrel it away against unforeseen troubles? Or did you look at it as a miracle waiting to happen? When the offering plate was being passed, did you ask yourself if God really needed your last $10 bill? Of course He didn't need your money. He owns a herd of cattle that would boggle the mind of a Texas millionaire rancher. Our Father's diamond mines make the

De Beers' conglomerate look like glass shards on the kitchen floor. And His diamonds really do last forever.

So what's the problem? If that $10 is your last cash, and you have no idea when and where your next paycheck is coming from, don't you need the miracle He has in store for you? If He's urging you to "think outside your box" and give to someone who needs it more, what keeps you from taking that leap of faith? You can trust Him to do what He says. "I have never seen the righteous forsaken or their children begging bread."

"But," you say, "that's all the money I have to my name. I have no way of getting any more between now and the end of the month." Not true! Not true! With the Creator as our personal Underwriter, no re-born child in God's universe ever lives on a fixed income. The Father's natural law is true, whether we're discussing dollars or daffodils.

In the springtime, a front yard down the road from mine is ablaze with yellow—daffodils. I feel compelled to praise God whenever I drive past. Years ago, some faithful gardener took the time to plant each bulb. Each spring her harvest blesses everyone who passes. She planted daffodils, not tulips, and she reaped daffodils, not tulips.

You and I reap what we sow. I've seen my daughter and son-in-law cheerfully give their last $20 to a homeless person and within days be blessed tenfold. Lois, an unemployed, single mother, faithfully gave God her last money and reaped incredible results. Remember the widow's mite? Not knowing what happened next, you might think, "that poor woman." Not so. One day she and her modern-day sisters will regale all of heaven with the "rest of the story," as radio commentator Paul Harvey would say.

The same God who set into motion the laws of gardening—plant sunflower seeds, reap sunflowers—promises to care for His own. If you give to those in need, your generosity will return to you. Giving to others spawns contentment, no matter who you are. When the Father says, "Be content with what you have," He's handing you your very own Heavenly Express Card. So what's in your spiritual wallet today? More than you think. And please, don't leave home without it.

Paul talks about the contentment that is ours in his first letter to Timothy: "Godliness with contentment is great gain. For we brought nothing into the world, and we can take nothing out of it" (1 Timothy 6:6, 7).

In these verses, the apostle directed his protégé's attention away from material things and toward eternal blessings. "I have learned to be content whatever the circumstances. . . . I . . . have plenty" (Philippians 4:11, 12).

Incarcerated in a Roman prison, Paul was giving an update on his personal well-being to the people of Philippi, who were supplying his physical needs. He was assuring them that his daily needs were being met and that he was pleased and content with their efforts.

When Richard and I began our teaching careers in Christian boarding schools, finances were tight. Our first on-campus home was an early twentieth-century, three-bedroom Craftsman home. We soon discovered that our draperies rippled in a breeze coming, not through open windows, but through the cracks in the molding. As to insulation in the walls or ceiling, there was none. A year later, when we moved out of the cottage and into a '50s ranch-style house on campus, the Dorcas Society moved in—for a year. Then the building was condemned by the state.

At the end of our first January in the place, we received, instead of a paycheck, a $300 bill for heating oil. Fortunately, we had a loving dad who believed in our ministry and bailed us out with a short-term loan. (There's a lesson in that, too, isn't there?)

On Sunday afternoons we would "knife" nickels out of a glass coin bank to treat ourselves to Fudgesicles to enjoy while driving through the foothills of the Appalachian Mountains. At that time fuel for our VW bug cost twenty cents a gallon and each Fudgesicle, one nickel. Yet we were content, even joyful. We were young, we were in love, and we believed we were where God wanted us to be, doing what He wanted us to do.

My favorite illustration of contentment is found in Habakkuk 3:17, 18: "Though the fig tree does not bud and there are no grapes on the vines, though the olive crop fails and the fields produce no food, though there are no sheep in the pen and no cattle in the stalls, yet I will rejoice in the LORD, I will be joyful in God my Savior." Habakkuk had learned the truth about rejoicing—it has nothing to do with what you do or do not have, or who you are, or where you are, or how gifted you might be. Praise and rejoicing are an emphatic choice. "Yet I will rejoice in the Lord!"

In the years following that first year of academy teaching, I've been content with little; and at times, discontent with much. For me, and perhaps it is true for you, contentment hasn't been a natural gift or a talent, but a skill to be learned—and occasionally forgotten. Many times upon seeing our monthly bills spread out on the kitchen table, I've thought, *If we only had a $50.00 buffer each month, we could make it.* The $50.00 lament has grown to, *If only we had another $100* . . . Unlike Habakkuk, and no matter how small or big our monthly checks might be, Richard and I have often found ourselves wishing for a "little more."

How discontent is my discontent? Recently a friend and I were discussing whether we would swallow live mealy worms, garden slugs, or the other vermin as do the participants on "reality" TV programs. When she wondered aloud how anyone could do such a thing, I remarked, "People will do a lot for a million dollars."

"Yes," she replied, "but a million dollars isn't as much as it used to be."

Humorous? Yes, but true. While a million dollars is still a million dollars to me, would I eat a cockroach for it? I'm not sure. A few years ago, a TV jingle asked, "What would you do for a Klondike™ bar?" Would you make a fool of yourself for an ice-cream sandwich? What would you do to win a state lottery? Have you ever fantasized on how you would spend your Reader's Digest sweepstakes winnings—after taxes, tithe, and offerings had been deducted, of course? Most of us have.

People get squirrelly over money, Christians included. Money can ruin the best of relationships. An acquaintance of mine won the Washington State lottery. I was surprised when she confided, "Winning has brought me nothing but trouble. You wouldn't believe the number of relatives who no longer speak to me because I couldn't meet all their financial demands. By the time I paid my taxes and paid off my credit cards . . ." And the list goes on.

Robert Bolt's play *A Man for All Seasons* includes the boast, "Every man has his price." Think about that for a minute. What would you do for an ice-cream bar or winning the lottery? Could you be satisfied with one million, ten million, or three hundred million dollars? Would enough ever be enough? If God can't trust you and me with a stained, wrinkled scrap of paper called a dollar bill, how can He trust us with the really valuable blessings stored in heaven's bank vault?

When I have out-of-town speaking engagements, I always return home with gifts for my grandsons—Jarod, age five and Alec, age two. It is understood that after one trip Jarod will choose first and after the next, Alec gets first choice. However, no matter which grandson makes the first choice or what that gift may be, the second boy always covets his brother's gift. It's inevitable. As the old saying goes, "The grass is always greener . . ." What we don't have always seems more desirable than what we do have. Understanding the humans He created, God advised us how to be happy: "Be content with what you have."

Our wise Creator knew that when His child's attention was focused on acquiring more "stuff," he would never crave the most valuable treasures, the riches of heaven. In the midst of our greed, He reminds us, "Seek ye first the kingdom of God, and his righteousness; and all these things shall be added unto you" (Matthew 6:33, KJV). To possess the priceless blessings of peace, joy, faith, and love, we must trust God to take care of the less important areas of our lives—money, cars, clothing, food—by living contentedly with the means He supplies.

While the word *contentment* refers to our personal possessions in which we can never find complete satisfaction, the word *satisfaction* applies to our eternal hunger. Within the psyche of every human being God has placed a dissatisfaction that causes an individual to yearn for an existence beyond his daily lot, to desire to seek after the Unknown. Unfortunately the farther we wander from our Creator, the more likely we will interpret this "hole in the soul" as the need for more playthings, more exciting people, and wilder experiences. As a result we miss out on both true contentment and complete satisfaction.

Sensing a need for a closer connection with the Father doesn't assume there is something necessarily wrong with your present spiritual condition. It may be the Holy Spirit luring you into an even richer experience.

One way to tell the difference between discontentment and dissatisfaction in your heart is to determine the source of your hunger, or as "Deep Throat," the mysterious informant in the Nixon/Watergate investigations said, "Follow the money." What do you expect to get out of the experience?

Matthew 6:21 says, " 'Where your treasure is, there your heart will be also." Look beyond your desire for a two-week jaunt to Alaska or a PT Cruiser parked in your garage. Determine if you are assuaging your hunger for God with the bite-sized sugar highs that material possessions afford.

Examine your motives. For what reason do you desire a closer walk with God? James 4:3 warns, "When you ask, you don't receive, because you ask with wrong motives, that you may spend what you get on your pleasures." Why do you hunger and thirst after righteousness? Why do you want an out-of-this-world experience with Him? Do you want a more visible connection with God so that others will envy your spirituality? Do you yearn to be known by your neighbors as the "woman whose prayers are always answered" or the "man who knows God's will"? Do you want something more to talk about at Wednesday night prayer meetings or a testimony to celebrate before the masses? After questioning your motives for desiring more of God, follow your heart.

I've always been a treasure seeker. What can be as exciting as uncovering a lost mine or hidden cache of riches, whether it be aboard a Spanish galleon off the coast of Florida or the Lost Dutchman Mine in Arizona?

Each Monday morning, treasure hunters methodically walk in a grid pattern on California beaches, skimming hand-held metal detectors across the sand. During weekend beach parties, people accidentally drop coins and jewelry. A quarter here, a half-dollar there; an ankle bracelet here, an engagement ring there—these industrious fellows make a good living scouring the beaches for treasures.

In my enthusiasm for finding the "big strike," I never thought much about the smaller treasures that might be lying about my feet. The same can be true for becoming aware of the essence of God's presence in your life. Begin by asking God to open your eyes to the heaven-sent treasures already scattered at your feet—a promise here, a blessing there, a rainbow here, a rosebud there, for "where your treasure is, there your heart will be also."

GRACE NOTES

- Begin a God-journal, noting the everyday blessings around you: a friend's smile; the moisture felt on your cheek from a child's kiss; a sip of icy lemonade a hot day; a gentle breeze stirring a wind chime outside your kitchen door; an unexpected thank-you email from a friend; a random act of courtesy in the checkout line. Give credit where credit is due; to the Father of all good things.
- Paraphrase Habakkuk 3:17, 18 with a list of your personal adversities. For example: "Though the bank didn't record my paycheck correctly; though the dishwasher is corroding my silverware; though my three children are sick with an intestinal flu and I'm not feeling too well myself; though . . ." You take it from there.
- When you finish, burst out with a loud and raucous psalm about stubborn rejoicing. If this exercise doesn't bring a chuckle to your lips and a smile to your heart, nothing will. Rejoice! Remember it's your choice to rejoice!
- Begin your own TV Guide, not a schedule of television programs but a reminder of your daily life. Write down every positive occurrence that is scheduled to happen in your day. Then check off the blessings as they occur. Add to your schedule the "To Be Determined" programs—every prayer answered and every unexpected pleasure enjoyed. You'll run out of space and time before God runs out of blessings.
- Make a list of all the things in your life that you most treasure. Since all good gifts come from the Father of lights, thank God for each of the items on your list. Next cross everything off the list that would lose its importance should you be told that you have only five days to live. Thank God for your revised list.

DYING OF THIRST

Come, all you who are thirsty, come to the waters
(Isaiah 55:1).

One of my favorite Scripture texts has been turned into a praise chorus. "As the deer pants for the water . . . so pants my soul for You, O God" (Psalm 42:1, NKJV). Singing the words, I picture myself as a spiritual Bambi, cavorting in a grassy meadow with my forest friends Thumper and Flower. A bit dry from our frolic in the sunshine, the three of us amble over to a sparkling brook, where we drink our fill of the fresh mountain water.

However my idyllic vision changed after I explored the word *pant*. *To pant* means "to long eagerly" and the context suggests extreme thirst. "As the life of a deer depends upon water so our lives depend on God. Those who seek Him and long to truly know Him will find eternal life. Feeling separated from God the Psalmist wouldn't [couldn't] rest until he had restored his relationship with God because his very life depended upon it." Psalm 42:1, Life Application Bible.

This psalm was written by the descendents of Korah, the priest who, with coconspirators Dathan and Abiram, was executed for rebelling against Moses. History tells us that Korah's offspring remained faithful and continued serving God in the temple as temple musicians.

That bit of history is encouraging. It would be a mistake to imagine that if the father's sin is visited "unto three and four generations," there is no room for genuine forgiveness and "moving on." On the contrary, Psalm 42 assures us that regardless of past mistakes, even in the face of blatant rebellion, God has a place for the repentant sinner and for his heirs.

The psalm's three-part structure—the call to worship, a confession of sin, and an encouragement to trust God—is God's antidepressant for today's woes, a solution for overcoming one of the most common and debilitating ailments of contemporary men and women—depression. The psalmist encourages the listeners to take their minds off their problems by drinking in God's unblemished record of goodness toward His children.

The psalmist David also wrote about the extreme thirst he experienced while hiding from his enemies in the Judean wilderness. "O God, you are my God, earnestly I seek you; my soul thirsts for you, my body longs for you, in a dry and weary land where there is no water" (Psalm 63:1).

The Old Testament has more than one word for water. The Hebrew term *mayim* is the most common. In Genesis 1:2, "the Spirit of God moved upon the face of the waters" (KJV). Genesis 26:19 uses it to describe living water as water that flows. Isaac's servants searched for and found a well of living water, fed by an artesian spring.

The "still waters" of Psalm 23:2 represent rest and peace to the traveler. In Job 9:30, *mayim* is used to describe water from melting snow. In Israel's temple rituals, *mayim* is the water used for purification. (See Leviticus 1:9 and Numbers 5:17.)[1]

God is in the business of purifying. I like that. When either of my grandsons gets a scratch or cut, I rush them to the sink and wash the wound with clean water. Of course the next step includes kisses and adhesive bandages decorated with cartoon characters. But the cleansing of the wound is paramount to its healing.

Another Hebrew term for water is *rhom*. *Rhom* implies deep water, the ocean, the earth's water tables, even flood waters. Psalm 107:26 says, "They mounted up to the heavens and went down to the depths [water]."[2]

Several years ago a young friend of mine was lamenting the "lukewarm" condition in many churches. The young man compared the church members to a river. He said, "What the church needs are young, energetic members to make things happen. Youth are like the swiftly moving current of water rushing down the center of the river. That's what keeps the water from becoming stagnant." He went on to observe, "Nothing seems to be happening in churches. We have too many older members content to lounge in the river's quiet eddies."

For the sake of debate, I reminded him that "a lot of babble from the fast moving water is merely snow runoff—here today, gone tomorrow. Silent waters run deep. While we might need the babble and enthusiasm of youth, the church also needs the stabilizing maturity of Christians who regularly drink from the deeper Living Water."

We were both right, and we were both wrong. Without the fervor of youth, a church truly is dying. It saddens me to visit a congregation where there are no children to come forward for a children's story. Yet without older, wiser sisters and brothers who regularly drink from the deep waters of God's Word, the church quickly becomes so much superfluous babble.

Age has little to do with spirituality. There is no righteousness by senility (a phrase coined by Pastor Morris Venden) or righteous by frenzy (that one's mine), but all righteousness comes only through Jesus Christ. I've met chronologically young Christians who drink deeply at the "Well," and I know silver-haired visionaries with wrinkles and age spots who exude the enthusiasm of new love in Christ.

Consider my ninety-plus-year-old friend Minnie. When I ran into her at the Washington camp meeting, the twinkle in her eyes and the praise on her lips looked and sounded more like that of a twenty-two-year-old bride. When I asked her how she was doing, Minnie answered, "Super, Kay, super. God is so good. This is my eighty-fifth camp meeting. Can you believe it? Praise His holy name."

The woman appeared younger than the last time I'd seen her. I had to urge her to tell me about the debilitating pain she suffers from rheumatoid arthritis and the recent death of her youngest son. Minnie's secret lies in the "Water" she drinks—not in her age.

The Spanish explorer Ponce de León set out from Cuba in search of the fabled Fountain of Youth. His quest took him north to what is now St. Augustine, Florida. But alas, he never found his enchanted spring. He died, never having drunk one drop of the mystical waters. You and I, regardless of our age, our past, our financial or educational circumstances, our sense of adventure, or our level of energy can find a fresh vitality and zest for life by drinking deeply of God's Fountain of Eternal Youth—the Bible.

Medical scientists have discovered that there is a direct connection between clinical depression and the eventual onset of osteoporosis in women. Surprise! Isn't that what the wisest man who ever lived said? "A cheerful heart is good medicine, but a crushed spirit dries up the bones" (Proverbs 17:22).

Good advice, don't you think? But one might ask, Is overcoming pain simply a matter of banishing negative thoughts or replacing negative thoughts with positive ones? Mind over matter? Distract yourself like you might distract a young child? Not quite. While that might work for visiting the dentist or for enduring an IRS audit, for the big stuff—life's sudden traumas—a distraction is not enough. Addicts have been trying that for generations. Alcoholics toss off another shot, hoping to escape their problems. Users take another snort of cocaine; smokers light up another cigarette in search of one delicious moment of peace. Dysfunctional sex addicts cruise the streets or the Internet in search of newer, younger diversions.

In contrast, when a Christian chooses to change his focus, he changes it from his problem to the Problem Solver—not to another problem. That's the only change of focus that is lasting—from the pain in your pocketbook or in your heart to the Creator of all things, to the One who promises to meet all your needs.

Have you ever tried to balance a straight broom by turning the broom upside down and placing the handle in the palm of one hand? As a child, I quickly learned that if I wanted to successfully balance the broom, I couldn't watch the point where the broom touched my hand, as instinctive as it may be to do so. To keep the broom balanced, I had to look up to the top of the broom.

Balancing straight brooms and balancing life's knottiest problems are similar. By concentrating on whatever difficulty is currently touching my life, I lose my sense of balance. To restore temporal balance, I must look away from the point where the problem touches my life. To restore my spiritual balance I must shift my attention from my problem to my Problem Solver. Jesus said, "Cast all your cares on Me." That's all—not some, not a few, not many—but all!

Both the deer panting for water and the broom balancer need a solution for very real problems. While we may thirst for God in life's good times, we pant for Him during turmoil. The soul's thirst can be quenched only by turning to Christ, the Living Water.

In the small town of Sychar lived a cheap trollop, you know the type, the woman scorned for her poor taste in clothing and her demeaning lifestyle. The woman recognized her thirst for water and set out to satisfy it, but not until after the good church ladies of Sychar had left the well. Early in the morning, the respectable townswomen had shared the hottest local gossip while filling their water jugs at the town well. They would wait until the worst of the heat had passed before making their second water run of the day.

But not our "soiled dove." She would do whatever it took to avoid the censorious glares from the good ladies of her community, even if it meant lugging her water jugs to the well and back again during the worst heat of the day.

Expecting to find the well at the edge of town deserted, the woman was surprised to find a stranger there, and even more surprised when He asked her for a drink of water. For Him to speak to her, regardless of His thirst, was unbelievable. She had to have asked herself, *What is He up to?*

The creature had three strikes against her. First, she was female. Respectable Jewish men never spoke with women in public, not even their own wives. The moral code of the Hebrew fathers decreed, "Don't waste your time speaking with women; and if this applies to your own wife, so much more to the wives of others. . . . Anyone who speaks much with women does himself harm, he ends up acquiring hell."[3]

Second, she was a Samaritan. No proper Jew, male or female, would speak to a person of her heritage. Even using a drinking vessel handled by a Samaritan would make a Jew ceremonially unclean. It would take several generations of "Jewishness" to cleanse her lineage of such impurities.

And third, she was a kept woman. If decent, law-abiding citizens of Sychar saw an upstanding Jew speaking to the likes of her, what would they think? Is He ignorant of who and what she is? Can't He see her shame? Is this a pick-up? It would be the end of His ministry in that region!

Definitely the smart response from her would be to ignore the Man and scurry home with or without the desired water. But she didn't. Perhaps it took a woman of her questionable virtue to break society's rigid rules.

"You are a Jew and I am a Samaritan woman. Why are you asking me for a drink?"

A wry smile must have crossed the Master's face as He read her thoughts. "If you only knew the generosity of God and who I am, you would ask Me, and I would give you living water."

His answer must have flustered her for a moment. "But, sir, you don't have a rope or a bucket. This well is very deep. Where would you get this living water?" I imagine that her voice was filled with sarcasm. "Besides, are you greater than our ancestor Jacob who dug this well and drank from it?" Sarcasm had become her only protection against society's barbs. "How can you offer better water than enjoyed by his sons and his cattle?"

The New Testament term for the Stranger's reference to "living water" referred to a natural artesian well. The living water to which the Stranger alluded was more desirable water, since Jacob's well (Genesis 33:18, 19) was fed by rain and dew that seeped into the bottom, and was not spring fed.

"Everyone who drinks this water will get thirsty again and again," the Man said. "Anyone who drinks the water I give will never thirst again—not ever! The water I give will be an artesian spring within, gushing fountains of endless life." When Jesus claimed to be able to give her living water to forever quench her thirst, He was announcing Himself to be the Messiah, the Promised One.

This analogy was familiar to Jews and Samaritans alike. In Psalm 36:9, the Savior is called the "fountain of life." He is called the "fountain of living waters" in Jeremiah 17:13 (KJV). While the woman failed to acknowledge the eternal truth the Stranger was sharing with her, she did recognize a good thing when she heard it. Imagine not ever having to scurry along the back streets of town to avoid the godly gossips whenever she needed a pail of fresh water. For whatever reason, her life hadn't gone as planned.

"Sir! Give me this water so I won't ever get thirsty, won't ever have to come back to this well again!" Can you hear the desperation in her voice?

God's presence at the well that day was not a human accident or the result of dumb luck. Hallelujah! Jesus' presence at that well, on that day, at that moment in history was part of a Divine plan formed before Creation itself. The Savior had a lesson to teach that would punch through time, down to us, and beyond. While His Jewish brothers might purposely skirt the "unclean" region of Samaria to avoid such awkward situations, the Savior chose to take the less-traveled road.

Living constantly in His Father's presence, Christ waited beside this well for the very purpose of meeting this woman—this woman who lived with a man who didn't love her enough to give her his last name, this woman who encountered the Promised Messiah despite His dusty garments, face, and beard; this woman who would immediately become, without hesitation, a missionary to the people who scorned her.

Every moment of every day on this earth, Jesus lived in His Father's presence. We don't need to know every step of God's plan to live every moment of our lives in the Father's presence, to be a part of His eternal plan for us. Is it merely good luck when you narrowly avoid a car accident or a stroke of bad luck when you don't?

The word *luck* is said to have been derived from the name Lucifer. It does ring of the happenstance of events credited to the father of chaos, and not to the Creator of eternal order and design. God's children aren't lucky; we're blessed. We're not flukes or serendipitous accidents. We're not pawns pushed here and there by spinning a wheel or drawing lots.

We are creatures of Divine design. Every detail of our lives was foreseen by our Father before the world was created. And every step we take can be guided by His love. That's living in His presence.

Living beautifully in the essence of God's presence begins by trusting that our lives are in the loving Father's hands. That, while the faithful child of God might not understand the reason for the good or bad moments that occur, we can know for certain that our lives aren't a series of accidental encounters, chance happenings, lucky or unlucky breaks.

The day the woman of Sychar met the Master, her thirst was quenched, her sins forgiven, and her wounds healed. God used a "fallen woman" to break His message out from behind the restrictive walls of Judaism. Later He would use another "fallen woman" to announce His triumph over death and sin—Mary Magdalene. The truth set both women free. The truth will set you free from the circumstances in your life, the conditions that are holding you back from completely trusting Him. The water He offered the woman of Sychar He offers freely to you and to me, today.

That God uses water to illustrate His forgiveness, mercy, and grace is no mystery. As one inspired writer put it, "In health and in sickness, pure water is one of heaven's choicest blessings.... It is the beverage which God provided to quench the thirst of animals and man. Drunk freely, it helps to supply the necessities to the system and assists nature to resist disease. The external application of water is one of the easiest and most satisfactory ways to regulate the circulation of the blood. A cold or cool bath is an excellent tonic. Warm baths open the pores and aid [the body] in the elimination of impurities. But warm and neutral baths soothe the nerves and equalize the circulation."[4]

This was written long before daily showers or baths were the norm. For those of us living in developed countries during the twenty-first century, running water is hardly a miracle, yet its healing properties remain a mystery and a delight. Water is available by turning on the tap. With every hot shower we enjoy, consider what Henry VIII, Cleopatra, or King Midas would have given for such a convenience.

Water allows us the freedom to revisit the child in us. Playing in water creates moments of heightened awareness. It calms, soothes, and stimulates our imaginations, all at the same time. It is said that Einstein developed his "theory of relativity" while shaving in his bathroom.[5]

Is it any wonder God uses the analogy of "living water" to describe the restored youth, renewed health, and effervescent vigor found when we allow the Holy Ghost to saturate us inside and out with His refreshing presence? If you hunger to live in the presence of God, if you yearn to intimately know the Father's heart, if you desire passionate encounters with the Savior, "Come all who are thirsty." You will find contentment. He will satisfy your cravings for more of Him.

GRACE NOTES

- Take a cooling or warming shower. Let the water rush over you. Feel it caress your skin. Taste it with your tongue. See it sparkle; hear it splash. Laugh out loud. Sniff its clean, fresh aroma. Rejoice in it. Praise the plumbers and the contractors who made it possible for you to enjoy this moment in the privacy of your home. Sing a hallelujah or two. Then, in humble gratitude, ask the Creator who endowed your body with a myriad of delightful senses and feelings to make you squeaky clean again—inside and out.
- Fill a tumbler with water. Hold it up to the light. Study the liquid's clarity, give thanks for its purity, and then drink it. Drink several more glasses. Feel it fill the empty void inside of you; feel its life-giving power rehydrate the cells in your body. Even as the planet's water table becomes more and more contaminated, He promised that your bread and water would be sure. Thank Him again for the always pure and clear living water available through His Son, Jesus Christ.
- Give thanks for your lot in life and your time and place in the plan of the universe. Recognize that you have been blessed by the King of all creation. You are wealthier than King Solomon. You have more power than a Titan. Ask your Father to show you how you can use the good and the not-so-good in your everyday life to glorify His holy name.

PLAYING HIDE-AND-SEEK

You will seek me and find me when you seek me with all your heart
(Jeremiah 29:13).

How audacious it sounds for human beings to seek the face of God. Moses sought God's face and, for his safety, was allowed but a glimpse of the Creator's back. What about you and me—can we seek the face of God?

Popular Eastern thought claims that "man is a spiritual being on a human journey." As poetic as that may sound, the opposite is true. We are human beings on a spiritual journey. God designed us to be human beings—creatures made to look like and act like Him. Genesis describes God walking in the Garden, enjoying His new creations.

Look over there! See Adam. He's trying to train a koala bear to fetch macadamia nuts. And there to the left, Eve is transplanting cuttings for her newest strain of lavender. Their fiftieth day together is coming to an end. The sun is reclining on the horizon. In minutes the Garden will be clothed in the caressing coverlet of night.

Adam looks up from his task and points toward the horizon. "Look, Eve. It's time!" Excitement fills his voice. "He'll be here any minute. Let's go meet Him."

"Oh my. I didn't realize it was so late. Wait for me!" The exquisitely beautiful crown of God's creation leaps to her feet, brushes soil off her robe of light, and hurries to her partner's side.

"I wouldn't leave without you, Sweetie." He laughs and grasps her hand in his. Together the two childlike beings scamper through patches of sunlight and shadows toward the Eastern Gate.

"I hope He tells us more about the personality of the tyrannosaurus. They're such big creatures and yet so gentle." Adam's eyes sparkle with anticipation.

"Look at this." Eve holds a large green rock up toward the sunlight. "Isn't it beautiful? I found it on the ground beside the granite cliffs. I just have to show it to Daddy. You know how much He loves beautiful things."

Eagerly they rush to meet their Creator, thus ending another day of their spiritual journey. Imagination? Yes. Scripture doesn't tell us how long the first couple lived in their beautiful Garden or how many visits they enjoyed with the Father before sin ruined their peaceful paradise. Scripture is silent as to whether or not the Son and the Holy Spirit also enjoyed these daily strolls through the royal test Garden.

But one evening as the sun dipped from view, the human couple didn't run to meet their Maker. Instead, they ran the other direction to the far side of the Garden, where long shadows from the sun hid them from view. There they quaked in fear of the One who had molded them from the dust, the One who had launched them on their spiritual journey, the One who would no longer be able to share the complexities of nature and the mysteries of the universe with them, face to face.

That evening, their spiritual journeys began a long detour from the adventure God would have preferred they take. They and their descendants would wander through arid wastelands; trek through tangled, tropical jungles; and wrestle the waves on wild and windblown oceans—all without the benefit of face-to-face meetings with their Maker.

Today it is sometimes hard for us to remember that we are children of the Royal Realm. Although we are scruffy, diseased, and blighted, we are God's creation, nonetheless. In the cosmic game of hide-and-seek, why would the Creator of the universe sit around and wait to be found?

My grandson Alec loves to play hide-and-seek. As any parent knows, the joy of playing hide-and-seek with a two-year-old is to hide in a place where he can find you. Knowing that I will always find Alec hiding in my walk-in closet and he'll always find me behind my office door doesn't diminish the excitement of our game. Squeals and giggles of joy erupt from both of us when either of us is "found." Following a twirl in Grandma's arms and a kiss on the cheek, Alec is ready to "hide" again from Grandma. When Alec tires of hide-and-seek, he knows that Grandma is eager to read him a story or give him a ride on her backyard prayer swing.

My grandson seeks me with his whole heart, all the while knowing exactly where he will find me. Should I choose to truly hide from him, I could hide in our attic. I could hide where he would never think to look. But what fun would that be? The fun is in the finding—sharing that tingly moment of surprise and joy.

I remember hiding once where my friends would never think to look—inside my father's tool closet in our garage. I waited and waited to be found, but no one opened the heavy wooden garage door. Eventually I grew impatient and abandoned my hiding space only to discover that my playmates were no longer searching for me or for anyone else. They'd gone to a friend's house for Popsicle® treats.

If you want to compare God's relationship with His kids to playing a game of hide-and-seek, you may. But from what I've discovered about the God of the Bible, He would never choose to hide where a two-year-old Alec or a fifty-nine-year-old grandma couldn't find Him. My loving heavenly Father also knows that the joy is in the finding. Throughout the universe, He leaves traces of Himself for us to find. His fingerprints can be seen wherever His children choose to look.

A similar game analogy might be track-and-trail. I attended grades one through seven at a school held in a room behind our church sanctuary. The church's tiny backyard was a fine play area for short recesses, but at noon, there wasn't ample room to work off the wiggles of fifteen rambunctious children.

Our teacher's solution was to take us on a hike to the Oakwood Cemetery that overlooks the industrial city of Troy, New York. There, during our lunch break, we would play track-and-trail in the woods surrounding the cemetery. Our game went like this: The older children had fifteen minutes to mark a chalk trail of arrows through the woods. At the end of the fifteen minutes, they would hide and wait for our teacher and the younger children to follow their chalk marks. I can still remember the mounting excitement I felt hunting for and finding the marks on tree trunks and rocks, directing us to where the older children were hiding.

When I look at the world God created, I see "chalk marks" along the way to guide me—"chalk marks" in His Word, "chalk marks" in the lives of my brothers and sisters in Christ, and "chalk marks" in the big, wide, more-than-wonderful natural world around me.

Consider the "chalk marks" King David refers to in Psalm 8:3, 4. "I look up at your macro-skies, dark and enormous, your handmade sky-jewelry, moon and stars mounted in their settings. Then I look at my micro-self and wonder, Why do you bother with us? Why take a second look our way?" (The Message).

Whether I'm hiking across desert sand or climbing a rocky cliff; whether I'm beachcombing at the ocean or standing in the middle of my postage-stamp-sized backyard, I look up toward the night sky and become giddy with excitement at the breathtaking fingerprints I see, evidence of God's majesty and love.

Imagine the massive power He has at His fingertips. Just imagine. If you could heat a straight pin to the core temperature of the sun, it would kill every man, woman, and child on planet Earth. The same sun has the equivalent of four trillion-ton hydrogen bombs continuously exploding on its surface. Talk about power! No energy shortage with Him. Yet the Creator has so finely tuned the distance between planet Earth and the sun that we experience appropriate warmth instead of total annihilation.

Think about this: You are standing motionless on the equator, yet you are traveling in six different orbits at the same time. First, the world is twirling at 1,000 miles per hour. The earth is circling the sun at 66,500 miles an hour. Simultaneously, the solar system (i.e. sun, earth, and other planets) is revolving around the hub of the Milky Way galaxy at approximately 500,000 miles per hour. The Milky Way, in turn, is moving about the core of galaxies at 1,350,000 miles an hour. In addition, the Milky Way is moving outward from this core at 360,000 miles per hour. Even the most advanced computer would crash attempting to calculate the God-sized numbers involved in all these sets of movements. Yet the Creator keeps that sum on the tip of His tongue, available at a moment's notice.

Isaiah expresses the gap between our ability and God's ability this way: " 'My thoughts are not your thoughts, neither are your ways my ways . . . [for] as the heavens are higher than the earth, so are my ways higher than your ways and my thoughts than your thoughts' " (Isaiah 55:8, 9).

In the world of numbers, consider the hairs on your head. God did in His design plan. He didn't plant your hair in a random willy-nilly fashion, a patch of twenty here, a clump of seventy there. He laid out a definite pattern in which your hair would cover your head.

Starting at your crown—the spot on top of your head from which your hair spirals (some people have double crowns)—the hair grows in a precise number pattern—1, 1, 2, 3, 5, 8, 13, 21, 34, 55, 89, 144. The numbers increase by adding the two numbers previous to get the next number—1+1=2, 2+1=3, 3+2=5, and so on.

Leonardo Fibonacci of Pisa, Italy, discovered God's unique number sequence in the thirteenth century. This is called the Fibonacci number scale. The same interesting phenomenon can be found in pinecones, branches of a pine tree, leaves of a head of lettuce, pineapples, cabbages, artichokes, and the petals of a daisy and sunflower, to name a few. While not all numbers in nature are Fibonacci numbers, every natural number can be expressed as the sum of distinct nonadjacent Fibonacci numbers.[1]

The story of Fibonacci numbers is a story of pattern. As we look at the world, we will see order, structure, and pattern. The order we see provides a mental concept that we can then explore on our own. As we discover relationships in the pattern, we frequently find that those same relationships refer back to the world in some intriguing way.[2]

From Fibonacci numbers I learn that my Creator is a God of order and design, not random chance or chaos. This assures me that I am not a zero in God's sight. I'm not a speck of cosmic dust hurtling through space on a minuscule planet called Earth, but I am an integral part of His plan, just as He stated in Jeremiah 29:11.

Consider another incredible phenomenon of the universe, the black hole. Black holes are collapsed stars with the force to crush any hapless object trapped in its gravity. Should the sun become ensnared in a black hole's gravitational pull, it would be compressed to a two-mile radius. Planet Earth caught in the same force would be reduced to a half-inch radius. Every black hole in space has a line scientists refer to as the Event Horizon. One step over that invisible line, and the victim would be consumed.

What a pity that some of God's children fear they've gone so far from their Creator, fear that they've sinned such dastardly sins that they have stepped beyond eternity's event horizon, and are about to be crushed into Satan's blackest of black holes from which there is no escape.

By looking into the depths of the universe, we can more clearly see how our Creator always wins over the darkest sin, the vilest behavior, and the deepest pit of despair. Whether we go by the name of Osama bin Laden, Saddam Hussein, George W. Bush, Billy Graham, or _____ (fill in the blank), we've all sinned and come short of God's glory (see 1 John 1:8, 9). That's a fact! It's up to us to deal with it.

The God who loves me so much He would rather die than live forever in a perfect universe without me—that same God is able not only to step over the line of the Event Horizon, but also to have a tug-of-war with the most powerful black hole in the universe—and win. And so I can know that, thanks to His incredible love, God's Son stepped over sin's blackest line of demarcation and rescued me from my own path of destruction as well. Signed, sealed, and delivered for all eternity at Calvary.

From the most glorious galaxy in the universe to the tiniest cell of the human body, the fingerprints of His love are evident if only we'll look. Each of us has one trillion cells in our bodies. Each cell contains one trillion atoms. Each of those one trillion cells makes one trillion new cells every day.

Consider the human body's DNA, the uniquely individual map of life that determines eye color, the tilt of the nose, the shape of the face, and the length of one's toes. One five-foot-long strand of DNA contains 50 trillion base pairs. If someone could link all the DNA strands found in one person's body, they would stretch ten billion miles. So why do we marvel over Jesus' pronouncement that "the very hairs of your head are all numbered"? (Luke 12:6-8, KJV).

Consider how the human bone marrow produces 2,000,000 blood cells every second. The quantity of blood cells produced in one second would circle the equator four times. Unfathomable! Go back with me to the place before the world began, back to the drawing board of Creation. See God the Father, God the Son, and God the Holy Spirit gather around their massive architectural table. See them sketch out the design of the creatures They would make in Their image.

Can you hear Their conversation as the Trinity labors over the design of that miracle fluid called blood? When the first blood cell was but a formula in the minds of the heavenly Trio, They all understood that the Son would shed that blood for the remittance of my sins, of your sins. The same blood that races through the hearts of wanton murderers, drug dealers, and terrorists bent on mass-destruction would one day flow through the Savior's veins. Yet God created humankind anyway.

Imagine! One droplet of the blood that Jesus spilled on the cross of Calvary had your name on it. Another had mine. Without taking the metaphor too literally, can the greatest economist calculate the divine value of the blood that covered our sins? On the scales of eternity, how much does one blood cell weigh when it's the Savior's? Wherever we look at creation, the message reads the same. "God so loved . . . he gave . . . that whosoever [you, me, Osama] believeth in him should not perish, but have everlasting life" (John 3:16, KJV).

A friend with doctorates in Greek, Hebrew, Sanskrit, and two additional ancient languages, whose names I can't even remember, told me that the Greek root word for *perish* means "to self-destruct." Humans, left to their own devices, become suicidal terrorists, maybe not as dramatic or fiery as the ones who make the evening news, but lethal nonetheless. Infused with sin, humankind is not only bent on destroying ourselves, but we want to take others with us.

Have you ever wondered why drug, alcohol, and tobacco users seem compelled to pressure others to become enslaved to their noxious habits? If I'm eating a giant slice of gooey chocolate cake dripping with fudge-and-marshmallow icing, I won't be completely happy until my husband tries some too. Does it remind you of Mother Eve's self-destructive behavior? Good, bad, or indifferent, whether today was just a bad hair day or whether the barrage of life's hassles have reduced you to a quivering fur ball, God's incredible love is the only power that can rescue you from you, and rescue me from me. Hardly a game of hide-and-seek. Sounds more like a search-and-rescue mission, if you ask me.

GRACE NOTES

- Sing "How Great Thou Art" while staring up at the night sky. Don't worry about those around you who might hear you sing this love song. You're not singing to them anyway.
- Log on to <www.hubblesite.org> to view photos of spiral galaxies, the birth of stars, and the mysteries surrounding Orion. Celebrate the power of God by singing or listening to a CD of praise music.
- Use the fantastically playful gift of imagination God has given you to glide on the wings of an angel, through outer space, past the moon and the sun, past Saturn's rings, past Pluto, straight to the seat of the universe, God's throne. Bow before Him in awe of what He's done for you.
- Find Fibonacci's number scale on a pinecone or a head of lettuce. Thank God for the intricate design He used to make you and for His intricate plan of salvation.

WHO'S SEEKING WHOM?

The Almighty is beyond our reach and exalted in power
(Job 37:23).

Enough! No one doubts that God is an almighty, all-powerful Creator. As Job wrote, "The Almighty is beyond our reach." So why try? How can we think we are anything more than dust bunnies under God's couch or a hiccough in time?

God Himself asked Job, "Where were you when I laid the earth's foundation? Tell me, if you understand. Who marked off its dimensions? Surely you know! Who stretched a measuring line across it . . . while the morning stars sang together and all the angels shouted for joy? Who shut up the sea behind doors . . . when I said, 'This far you may come and no farther'?" (Job 38: 4, 5, 7, 8, 11).

Is it not audacious to think mere humanity could seek and find the Creator of the universe? Yes, without the element of God's love, it would be the height of audacity. From what I read in His Word, God isn't toying with humankind. Our eternal life and His everlasting love are issues too serious to be left to the fate of childish games.

The reality is that you and I aren't seeking God as much as He is continually reaching out to us in every way imaginable. From the cheerful greeting of the checkout clerk in the grocery store to the tiniest blossom peeking out from under a tangle of weeds in the garden; from the gentle rains of springtime to the glistening droplets of dew on a California poppy, God touches our lives with His love.

Better metaphors than kids' games might be the parables Jesus told to illustrate the Father's quest for us. Remember the story of the woman who lost a valuable piece of her dowry? The gold coin didn't know it was lost; it was just lost. Whether it was gold, silver, or copper, the coin didn't have a clue that it represented the economic worth of the frantic woman. If she were single, the loss of the coin diminished her value as a desirable marriage partner. If she were married, a husband could divorce her or "put her away" at will for such carelessness.

Jesus illustrates His search for us by depicting Himself as the desperate woman, searching for those who are lost and who don't even know they are lost. The custom of the bridal dowry was not divinely ordained, nor was it particularly Jewish. As the men of Israel took foreign women as wives, the customs of their neighbors gradually crept into the Hebrew lifestyle. In the post-biblical Jewish writings called *Midrash*, King Solomon is said to have married an Egyptian woman whose dowry included 1,000 musical instruments.[1]

Usually a bride's dowry was made up of coins, as in Christ's story. She might have worn her wealth as jewelry, or she might have stored it in a satin pouch or hand-carved chest. Where she stored her lost coin was immaterial to the story, as was how the treasure happened to become lost or even where it was eventually found. The point the Master Teacher wanted to make was how valuable the coin was to the frantic woman and how desperate her search for it illustrates in a small way God's search for us, who often don't even know we are lost.

Too many people today feel as if they are nothing but big, fat zeros. They see themselves as insignificant specks of useless lint in the fabric of the universe. They see themselves as nothing more than a step in an evolutionary process. Whenever they turn on the television or pick up a magazine, someone is there to point out their flaws, telling them they are useless unless they use Sparkle toothpaste or eat Crunchy Flakes cereal. To prove they are more valuable than their neighbors, they must be seen driving the latest luxury SUV or the swankiest sports car. Society's philosophy of personal value has nothing to do with character and everything to do with amassing toys.

Recently, while lamenting the lack of manners on the highway, my daughter Kelli pointed out that the turn signal is the only piece of equipment on a vehicle that is used solely as a courtesy to other drivers. No wonder so many drivers fail to use their turn signals. Why should they care about the other guy? Might makes right, right? Look out for number one! To prove your worth, get ahead at any cost.

The lost coin is descriptive of those of us who don't have a clue that there is a God who loves us. And regardless of how totally worthless we may feel at the end of the day, we are still of incredible worth to our heavenly Father. God, like the woman in the story, will delve into every trash bin and burrow under every layer of dirt in an attempt to reach our hearts.

In the story of the lost sheep, God reveals His love from another angle. In this parable the animal knew it was lost, but had no idea as to what to do about it. Perhaps in its search for greener grass, it wandered the opposite direction from the rest of the flock. And when the creature looked up from its patch of clover, the other sheep were nowhere to be seen. Neither was the shepherd. Suddenly the terrain looked foreign and the skies threatening. Quivering with fear, the sheep realized it was hopelessly lost. On its own, it would never find its way back to the safety of the fold.

In this illustration Jesus is again doing the searching. He's the Good Shepherd; I am His precious lamb. I like knowing that the shepherd in the story loved his one lost lamb so much that he left the other ninety-nine safely penned in for the night and trekked across hills and gullies until he found the errant animal and brought it safely home.

Scripture mentions sheep about 750 times. Sheep were well-suited for the area, but they were dependent on their shepherd. He led them to pasture, located water sources to quench their thirst, and protected them from wild beasts. A good shepherd cared deeply for his sheep. He not only knew how many were in his flock, but he called them by name. At night all the local shepherds' flocks would be penned together. Imagine the morning cacophony of voices as each shepherd called to his sheep. Yet the sheep recognized their own shepherd's voice and followed him.

Given the choice of being depicted as a creature other than a human, I doubt I'd choose to be compared to a sheep. Let me be a powerful eagle or a frolicking seal or perhaps a dancing dragonfly, but not a plodding sheep. While a newborn lamb may be cuddly and playful, a mature sheep is anything but.

To put it nicely, a sheep is an intellectually challenged creature. While visiting Stonehenge in England, I watched a shepherd lead his sheep along the outside perimeter of the fenced-in tourist area. The herd of sheep walked single file along the fence. Suddenly one of the animals stumbled and fell. Instead of walking around the fallen sheep, the remainder of the flock scrambled over him, trampling him into the dirt. That couldn't give an accurate picture of how humans often behave toward one another, could it?

Sheep make poor burden bearers. A horse can be trained to carry heavy packs, as can a camel, an ox, even a llama. But a sheep? When it comes to carrying burdens, sheep are useless, much like humans. Our shoulders and backs weren't designed to bear heavy packages. Instead, like sheep, we must trust the Good Shepherd to carry us on His shoulders. Another similarity is that we were created to be obedient followers (but not frightened, passive animals).

Can you imagine the shepherd, back at the fold, counting his sheep that night? "Ninety-seven, ninety-eight, ninety-nine…" He pauses to look around. Had he miscounted? Did the new spring lamb slip into the pen without his knowing? He counts his flock a second time. "… ninety-eight, ninety-nine …" He scrutinizes the animals present until he's certain that baby Philbert isn't in the pen. All day long the shepherd had chased after the capricious little creature. And now, he's missing! There is only one thing the shepherd can do—go back out into the darkness of night and find Philbert.

As the shepherd trudges over the rocky ground, calling Philbert's name, he can hear wolves howling in the distance. The shepherd tightens his hold on his trusty crook when he spots the skittering shadow of a predator—perhaps a bear or a lion. All night long He searches until he finds his errant Philbert, treats the creature's wounds, and carries the little lamb safely back to the fold. An interesting picture of a loving Shepherd searching for you and for me.

Some believe the story of the prodigal son should have been called "the story of the patient father." You recall the story. With his share of the family wealth stuffed in his pockets, the spoiled, ungrateful second son left home. Did the father know his son would squander the money? Of course. Did he know that his hard-earned cash would destroy the boy he loved so much? Absolutely. Yet he gave the riches to him anyway. Was he a wise father? Some may say No. Yet divine love says Yes.

Every day thereafter, the father searched the horizon for his wayward son. And every day he was disappointed. Do you think it was easy for the father to wait until his son came to his senses? If you've ever been a parent, you would know that waiting for a child to come to his senses takes an incredible amount of patience and love. I wonder how many times the father considered sending out his most trusted servants to find this son. Or better yet, how many times had he seriously considered going to the far country himself to find him?

Eventually, like the lost lamb, the son recognized he was lost. But unlike the lamb, he knew his way home. But before he could swallow his pride and admit he'd been wrong, the prodigal son had to become totally desperate. It's interesting that even after the son recognized his need and returned home, he still didn't really know or understand his dad or the extent of the father's love.

Obedience without love is slavery. The wealthy landowner wanted more from his precious child than blind obedience—even if it meant letting the son leave. Love demanded that the father give his child the space to turn away from his bad choice and to come to his senses. Anything less would not be love but arbitrary control—do it my way or else! The need to control comes to us from the father of lies, not from God, the Father of Light.

Sometimes this is hard for humans to understand. When troubles come, we blame God. We say foolish things like, "Why did You let this happen?"

Looking at the prodigal son story, the reason becomes clear—"For God so loved." Anything less than total freedom would not be love, and God is Love.

I especially like the part of the story where the joyous dad takes off his silken robe and wraps it around his son's soiled and sweaty shoulders. The boy had been living with swine and dining on swill. Not only is the father's gesture a graphic picture of loving the unlovely, but also of our loving, forgiving heavenly Father. This is also the reason the father scanned the road every day, hoping to catch a glimpse of his returning son. The law of the day declared that a wayward, disobedient son should be stoned at the city gates (Deuteronomy 21:18-21).

The loving father was determined that no one would kill his son, regardless of the boy's sins. His plan was to run to him the minute he saw the boy coming and wrap his robe about his son's shoulders. The father's robe not only covered the boy's shame, but declared to the city fathers, in no uncertain terms, "He's my son! You touch my boy; you touch me!"

The father's robe protected the young man against the just and legal punishment for his behavior. In the book of Ruth, Boaz's robe became her legal protection. Elijah gave his mantle to Elisha to delineate protection and authority as well.

I love the Judgment Day description of Christ draping His robe of righteousness around our guilt-burdened shoulders. As the entire universe observes the gesture, I can hear my Savior say, "Too bad, Satan! She's all mine!"

Where do you fit into God's search for His precious lost? The coin was lost and didn't know it; the lamb knew he was lost but didn't know what to do about it; the son both knew he was lost and knew how to find his way back home.

Too many doubt God's promises because they measure God's goodness and worthiness against their own. They believe value is in the eye of the beholder. Sea shells, coins, stamps, diamonds, and automobiles are only as valuable as others perceive them to be. The inestimable value of a human being to God is measured on an entirely different scale than the one used by humankind.

As a teenager, my husband collected baseball cards. He stored his set of perfect, mint-ten condition, 1950s collection in a shoebox under his bed. After he left for college Richard's mother, certain he'd outgrown his love for such childish stuff, tossed the cards, shoebox and all, into the garbage. In a flash, his Mickey Mantel, Joe DiMaggio, and Hank Aaron cards became ashes scattered over the East River.

A prime, mint-ten condition Mickey Mantel card would be worth thousands today. If you accidentally or otherwise bend one tiny corner of that card, its value would drop to a couple hundred dollars. Bent, folded, or scarred in any other way, and the value of the card plummets to a mere $20.00.

That's how the world sees you and me, the crown of God's creation—like collectables. The value of a collectable is determined by its appearance. In human terms, the value of the woman is determined by her beauty, her perfect appearance. When damaged, even slightly, her value drops precipitously. A man is more often measured by the bulge in his portfolio or the vehicle parked in his driveway or the price of the watch on his wrist.

But that's not how our Creator looks at us. Your and my value to God the Father can be compared to the way a bank teller sees a dollar bill. A United States minted bill can be bent, folded, crumbled into a ball, soiled with the filth of the street, but at the bank, the buck is still worth 100 pennies or 10 dimes, or 4 quarters. The cash value hasn't been affected by its ratty condition. The condition of the bill doesn't affect its worth. What affects the value of money is the power behind it—in the case of a dollar bill, the United States government.

Likewise our worth as human beings to the Father is never affected by how clean we've kept ourselves, how perfect we look, the number or seriousness of our sins, or how bent, crumpled, or mutilated we may become. Our worth is determined by the Power who stands behind us, Jesus Christ. Just as the official stamp of the United States government gives the dollar its value, so the stamp of the Savior's sacrificed blood determines your value and mine. Because God's love for us never changes, our value to Him remains constant, regardless of our condition.

However, as immeasurable as God's love for us is, it couldn't save us. Our salvation came with His death on the cross of Calvary. It is the sacrifice He made because of His love that grants us eternal life.

When my elder daughter was a toddler, she would hide in the pantry beside the kitchen door every afternoon, waiting for her daddy to come home. As he entered the house Rhonda would pop out of the pantry and into his arms. After a hug and a kiss, Richard would ask her, "How much do you love me?"

Rhonda would stretch out her little arms and say, "This much, Daddy. I love you this much. How much do you love me?"

Then Richard would stretch out his arms and declare, "This much! I love my little girl this much!" His stretch was much wider than that of his four-year-old daughter. So our Savior's stretch is much wider than yours and mine. Jesus Christ loved us so much that He stretched out His arms on a hand-hewn, Roman cross and died. The Creator of the universe couldn't love us more, and He wouldn't love us less.

So who's really doing the seeking—me or God? Perhaps it's a mutual search. I have a God-sized hole within me that only He can fill. And He has a place in His heart that is custom-made just for me. I need Him as much as He needs me. We both have an eternity worth of loving to lose and a universe of unbelievable joys to enjoy together.

While Job tells us that "the Almighty is beyond our reach and exalted in power" (Job 37:23), we are never, ever, ever out of His reach. And that makes all the difference. When you take one step in His direction, He will run to you.

GRACE NOTES

- From God's Word, read each of the four stories that illustrate God's search for you. Insert your name wherever the words *coin, lost sheep, prodigal son,* or *pearl* are mentioned.
- Recall a time when something you valued was lost and experience again the relief you felt when you found it. Thank God for leading you to it.
- Ask God to lead you to a person in need of your help. Meet their immediate need. Thank God for the privilege of being His hands and His feet.
- Recall a time when you were lost and alone. Which of the parables best described your situation? Praise God for His faithfulness in finding you.

GOD AND INFINITY

How exquisite your love, O God! How eager we are to run under your wings, to eat our fill at the banquet you spread as you fill our tankards with Eden spring water. You're a fountain of cascading light, and you open our eyes to light
(Psalm 36:7-9, *The Message*).

In this place, God is. Whether you are reading this book in your special place of prayer, curled up on your favorite sofa, seated at your kitchen table, or pacing a busy airport, God is not only with you, but the Holy Spirit is in you.

God is present in the room where you are sitting. He hears each breath you take, each sigh. He notes every smile that touches your lips. The essence of His presence is everywhere, from the deepest sea to the most distant galaxy at the edge of the universe.

He knows every thought flashing through every mind of the five billion people on planet Earth. He knows every thought we've ever had, every hurt we've experienced. Every bruise, scrape, scar, or tear, He knows and remembers—for all five billion of us.

God read the thoughts of Adolf Hitler when he conducted the most brutal annihilation of humankind in recorded history. He also sees you and me as we scheme to get ahead of our competition, whether we are on the highway, in the classroom, in the boardroom, or in His sanctuary. He sees all—and loves us anyway.

Listen to the poet's words.

Yahweh . . . I'm an open book to you;
even from a distance, you know what I'm thinking.
You know when I leave and when I get back;
I'm never out of your sight.
You know everything I'm going to say
before I start the first sentence.
I look behind me and you're there,
then up ahead and you're there, too—
your reassuring presence, coming and going.
This is too much, too wonderful—
I can't take it all in!

(Psalm 139:1-6, *The Message*).

When I was a teenager, the idea that God was everywhere and knew everything disturbed me. Call it a guilty conscience. Call it an adolescent's struggle to break free of parental restraints. I don't know. But I wanted my freedom and I wanted it then.

Being an adult in a world of chaos, I now find Psalm 139 comforting, especially after the day I received a call from my sister telling me that my mom had died. I remember Connie's agonizing cry, "Kay, we're orphans."

Orphans? The term sounded strange coming from a fifty-eight-year-old woman. But as the reality of my mother's demise took root in my brain, I too, cried to my heavenly Father, "O God, I'm an orphan!" There would be no more Mother's Day cards to purchase. There would be no parental arms to welcome me home. There would be no financial safety net in which to fall. There would be no "older generation" to turn to for wisdom and for comfort. I suddenly had become the "older generation." Me! How could I comfort; how could I become a fountain of wisdom when I still needed so much comfort and wisdom myself?

I could only cling to the promise that said I'd never ever be alone, that I could never be an orphan, that my heavenly Father would be my shelter, my security, my comfort wherever life might take me.

Is there anyplace I can go to avoid your Spirit?
to be out of your sight?
If I climb to the sky, you're there!
If I go underground, you're there!
If I flew on morning wings
to the far western horizon,
You'd find me in a minute—
you're already there waiting!
(verses 7-9).

I confess that I love to fly, preferably in an airplane. I have friends who hate to fly for any reason. They prefer speeding down a highway at 65 or 70 miles per hour in a glorified tin can. I have other friends who say hang-gliding and sky diving are a real kick and that I should try it. They're probably right, but I'm too chicken to try. Knowing my coordination, I'd break a leg or wrench an ankle, and that's assuming my parachute opened or my hang-glider didn't crash into the side of a mountain. Frankly, both extremes seem insane at times.

In my younger days, I tried flying without a plane, first at age five, down a flight of stairs; and second, at eight, from the roof of our kitchen. Both times I flew—for a short distance. And then gravity kicked in, and I firmly hit terra firma. Ouch! Yet I treasure the knowledge that someday I will fly (safely) on the wings of the morning. But until the Creator gives me my very own set of durable and aeronautically correct appendages, I'll do my flying in a Boeing 747.

The psalmist continues praising God's knowledge and presence:

You know me inside and out,
you know every bone in my body;
You know exactly how I was made, bit by bit,
how I was sculpted from nothing into something.
Like an open book, you watched me grow from conception to birth;
all the stages of my life were spread out before you,
The days of my life all prepared
before I'd even lived one day

(verses 15, 16).

Good, bad, indifferent—regardless of your mind-set, He loves you with an *agape* love. *Agape* love or "God-love" is a constant thing—present tense, whether you're talking about fifty years ago when you wore your hair in long, golden ringlets or fifty years later, when the hair on your head has gone south to your nostrils and chin. He loves you infinitely, for He is an infinite God.

Divide infinity in half and what do you have? Infinity. Divide infinity by the 6,500,000,000 inhabitants on planet Earth, and you still have the infinite love of God for you, the individual. He loves you infinitely as your Father, infinitely as your Brother, infinitely as your Best Friend, infinitely as your Master, infinitely as your Great Physician, infinitely . . . Think of all the metaphors God uses in His Word to describe the relationship He wants to have with you—Shepherd to His sheep, Potter to clay, Vine to the branches, Husband to His bride, Savior to the lost—the list goes on. Even before you gave your life to Him, the infinite God loved you, infinitely.

The symbol for infinity, a reclining eight, has no beginning and no end. If you brought a long, narrow strip of paper together, you'd have a loop. Before taping the ends together, make a half twist and you have a Möbius band.

What converts an ordinary loop into a Möbius band? It's the twist, of course. A simple half twist creates unexpected wonders. Take a red marker and draw a line along the length of the band until you get back to where you started. What was outside is inside, and vice versa. You can trace the red line around the loop as often as you like, and you won't come to an end. The Möbius band is infinite; it has no end. Imagine that God's love is the Möbius band and you are the red line. There is no end to the relationship.

Take the illustration one step further. If you cut the band along the center, you will end up with two loops, and neither will be a Möbius band. The only one who can separate you from God's infinite love is you. You must be the one to make the cut in the infinite Möbius band of God's love. Paul asks, "Who shall separate us from the love of Christ? . . . I am convinced that neither death nor life, neither angels nor demons, neither the present nor the future, nor any powers, neither height nor depth, nor anything else in all creation, will be able to separate us from the love of God that is in Christ Jesus our Lord" (Romans 8:35, 38, 39).

If nothing can separate you from the infinite reality of God's love, how can you become more aware of His presence in your daily life? His first command is to "love God with all your heart, soul, and mind." Love Him with all your energy and strength, with every thought and action, with every fiber of your being. That's a mighty tall order, but that's *agape* love.

You've experienced *agape* love if a tear enters your eye when you hold your firstborn for the first time. You've experienced *agape* love if a lump forms in your throat upon seeing your parents renew their wedding vows on their fiftieth anniversary. You've experienced *agape* love if you heart melts at the sight of your grandchild running to you with open arms. *Agape* love is a God-given love. It's a 1 Corinthians 13 kind of love. It's a love that doesn't spring naturally from a carnal heart. It's a love with no strings attached, no conditions, and no pre-nuptial clauses.

Loving someone in order to get something in return is never love. Inside or outside of the marriage relationship, it's prostitution. A woman named Betty* set her cap, as my grandmother would have called it, for a doctor or a preacher. When she landed her doctor, she wasn't marry-

---

*Not her real name.

ing the man, but his title. She savored the prestige that comes with being a doctor's wife. When she spoke of her husband in conversation with other women, she referred to him, not as Jim or even James, which was his name, but as "the doctor."

Unfortunately James or Jim or "the doctor" smashed into his midlife crisis with the force of an Indy 500 race car. Battered and disillusioned, he abandoned his practice to paint houses with his dad. Betty felt betrayed and humiliated. Jim was no longer the man she married. She'd sacrificed, scraped, and struggled to put him through medical school and residency. She buoyed his spirits when he'd wanted to quit. She'd pushed and prodded. She deserved better. After six months as the wife of a house painter, Betty walked away from the relationship. Years later when she told me her story, her voice was still filled with bitterness and anger.

Faith without love is cold; hope without love is hollow. You can't increase your faith by pursuing faith. You don't build hope by repeating a mantra every morning and evening. Love warms, softens, and illuminates. Love precedes faith and hope.

By contemplating God's infinite love, we can love beyond ourselves and our own needs—and by doing so, enter into the divine relationship He yearns to share with us. The more we think about how long, how wide, how high, how strong, and how deep God's love is and how like an ocean His forgiveness is, the more we want to run to Him. There is no place on the planet as safe and secure as snuggling down in the center of His infinite will.

The better we know Him, the more we'll love Him; the more we love Him, the better we'll know Him. The lyrics of a '50s pop song expressed the concept like this, "To know, know, know him is to love, love, love him." While the lyricist was speaking of human love, the same is true of Divine love. The more we know our Savior, the more we will love Him.

I like to listen to the Golden Oldies station while I'm riding in the car. It's like meeting up with old friends after a long absence. Richard will cast me the same glance that won my heart forty-two years ago, and

I am a love-struck teenager once more. I sigh, smile, and recall warm and fuzzy memories of poodle skirts, Ferris wheel rides, and kisses in the back seat of a turquoise and white '57 Chevy.

Occasionally an old-fashioned love song will come along with lyrics that I can sing directly to my heavenly Husband. It is surprising how many songs of the '50s, '60s, and '70s can celebrate an *agape* love as well. When I find one such song, the Holy Spirit speaks to my heart through the simple lyrics, and I am in the presence of my Eternal Beloved.

Solomon's Song of Songs is an exquisite love story about a Jewish maiden and her lover (Solomon, the king). Scholars theorize that King Solomon wrote it early in his life, before his sexual appetite had become jaded with overindulgence and self-gratification.

For centuries scholars have debated as to whether or not the book should be included in Holy Scripture. Theologians cannot agree as to its purpose and meaning. Is it a simple wedding song, honoring marriage? It certainly does that. Love couched in exquisite beauty and innocence, the book contains the most explicit sexual statements found in the Bible.

Is it a pastoral poem to be enjoyed for its literary value of love— God's choicest gift to His children—put into words? In God's Word, poetry is used to convey sacred truths through compression of ideas, thought-rhythm, picturesque imagery, and colorful figures of speech. The freshness and vigor of the poem engages the imagination and enables the message to linger in the memory.

Or is it a literal story, a dramatic dialogue about a happily married couple taking a legitimate delight in one another? The female speaker is called a "Shulamite" in chapter 6, verse 13. In it she refers to the man she loves as "my king" and "my beloved." Some scholars believe the word "Shulamite" translates as the feminine form of "Solomon." This would agree with the poem's presentation of the woman as Solomon's opposite and equal.[1]

The male speaker, King Solomon, refers to the object of his affection as "my love," "my bride," "my spouse," my dove," "my perfect one," and "my sister," a term of endearment for a lover that appears in other ancient Near Eastern poetry.[2]

The Song of Solomon is all of the above—a song to celebrate marriage, a pastoral poem, a moving story, and a dramatic dialogue between two lovers detailing their feelings for each other—and more. The historical story has two layers of meaning. One layer is the obvious story of love between a man and woman. On a deeper level, it becomes an allegory about God's overwhelming love for you and for me.

Scripture describes the marital union with the word *knew* (Genesis 4:1, KJV). How fitting to define the relationship God longs to have with you and me in the same intimate terms (Ephesians 5:31, 32). "Properly and ultimately there can be no separate chasm between love divine and love human; and because of this fact the marriage bond became, both in the Old Testament, and the New Testament, the symbol of the divine love."[3]

"Place me like a seal over your heart, like a seal on your arm; for love is as strong as death, its jealousy unyielding as the grave. It burns like blazing fire, like a mighty flame. Many waters cannot quench love; rivers cannot wash it away. If one were to give all the wealth of his house for love, it would be utterly scorned" (Song of Solomon 8:6, 7).

In the Song of Solomon, you will find no mention of God, the Savior, a sacrifice, temple, the priests or prophets, eternity, the Cross, religion in general, or any of the themes prevalent throughout the rest of the Bible. Could it be that the theology typically found in the other books of the Old Testament is absent for a reason? Is it possible that theology can get in the way of our falling in love with Jesus, our Bridegroom?

Some interpreters define the word *religion* as meaning "back to bondage." Jesus' mission to planet Earth was to break the bondage of religion, or human attempts over the centuries to reach God. The Savior came to establish a relationship of God reaching humankind, a love story to end all love stories.

The story line in the Song of Solomon can be broken down into three distinct views of God. The Shulamite woman first recognizes her king. This was the first view I had of God as well. I was overwhelmed by His majesty, His omnipotence, and His omnipresence. I fell at His feet to worship Him. I couldn't look at Him without recognizing how bad I was and how good He is. That seemed to be the extent of my faith in worship. But He didn't leave me there. The Lover of my soul wanted to take our love to the next level.

If all God had wanted from me was my obeisance, He could have stayed in heaven and sent fire and brimstone down on my head (and there were times I deserved it!). But the Creator of the universe didn't design me for that purpose. Little by little our relationship grew, and my faith increased until I stood in His presence.

Likewise, in Solomon's song, the king didn't leave the woman groveling at his feet, but came to her as a shepherd. He lifted her up, elevating her to the status of a friend. The young girl and her shepherd worked, laughed, and played side by side as friends.

So God, the Son came to earth to walk with humankind, to laugh, to cry, to hurt as they hurt, to become closer than a brother (Proverbs 18:24, KJV). The relationship is built on trust, day after day the act of proving One's devotion and faithfulness. Any marriage will be stronger if a couple learns to trust one another as friends before the wedding.

The friendship stage with our relationship with God is as vital to growing a healthy spiritual relationship as it is to growing a healthy marriage relationship. When God promises, "Never will I leave you; never will I forsake you" (Hebrews 13:5), He is giving His word. But if I don't know Him well enough to realize that He cannot lie and still be God, I may have doubts. It is only as I spend time with Him that I learn to trust Him to keep His word.

The third view of God found in the Song of Solomon is that of a lover. "I am my lover's and my lover is mine"—with all the exclusivity that entails. No one can be allowed to breach the protective walls of that love relationship, whether it is between a man and a woman or between a human being and God.

From the beginning of the book, "Let him kiss me with the kisses of his mouth—for your love is more delightful than wine. Pleasing is the fragrance of your perfumes; your name is like perfume poured out," to the book's finale, "Come away, my lover, and be like a gazelle or like a young stag on the spice-laden mountains," the couple's love doesn't end.

"God has bound our hearts to Him by unnumbered tokens in heaven and in earth. Through the things of nature, and the deepest and tenderest earthly ties that human hearts can know, He has sought to reveal Himself to us."[4]

God wants me to know Him as my Beloved. He already knows my inmost being, all the tiny intricacies that make me who I am (Psalm 139:13). In turn, He wants me to know Him too. He longs for me to build a love with Him that will last throughout eternity.

This God-love of which Solomon sang calls to you in every way possible, through every avenue. He uses all five senses as well as the place in your deepest heart of hearts. You know that you recognize His all-consuming power, His limitless majesty, His infinite love. And you long to know Him better.

God doesn't demand your presence. God is a perfect gentleman; He never forces Himself on anyone. Force is the devil's modus operandi. God waits for you to come to Him—freely, just as you are.

With each step you take closer to Him, you more clearly see your purpose for being. You better understand your value to Him. As He holds you close, He clears your vision; He heals your mind. In His presence you will begin to see yourself and your world through His corrective lenses. He will teach you to value the beautiful child hiding beneath the garbage sin has thrown at you.

There's an unexplainable essence that surrounds someone in love. We've all seen it. My mother and dad said they knew I'd "met the one" the moment I walked in the front door of our home. I stood taller, smiled wider, and carried myself with a new aura of grace. I was valuable. Someone loved me. His name was Richard.

Forty years later the essence is stronger than ever. I am alive to my husband's mood changes. Without a word, I know whether his day was good or bad, whether he feels extra tired or has an ache in his back. I thrill at the sound of his voice on the telephone. My heart leaps at the sight of him walking through the door at the end of the day. I still feel a tingle of joy when he takes my hand. I am moved by his presence.

I don't worry that I can't make a great pie. There's a great pie shop in the next town. I'm learning not to feel threatened when I see evidences of gravity working on my body. That's what it means to grow old together, right? I'm content loving a man who claims that neither a paintbrush nor a wrench fits comfortably in his hand.

A wise woman doesn't love her hubby because he has a Hummer II parked in the garage or because he once rescued her from an avalanche. She loves him for who he is—the lion of a man who loves her in return.

My husband loves me—and he loves hearing me tell him so, again and again and again. Whether I shout the words over the phone, signal to him from across a crowded room, or subtly remind him of my love with a batch of chocolate chip cookies, he never tires of hearing me say, "I love you."

God never tires of hearing "I love You," either. His heart is naturally drawn to you individually. While there are billions of others, His love for you is as personal as your fingerprints and your tongue print. And when you tell Him you love Him, you do so in your own unique fashion. No one can worship God exactly the way you do. And when you're too busy or distracted to express your love for Him, He misses it.

When you worship God with the passion found in the Song of Solomon, you will experience the most outrageous love connection possible in this life. More and more you will find yourself coming to Him for no earthly reason—no requests, no pleas, no complaints—but simply to praise and love Him. This is the purest form of worship.

I am moved by Mary's sacrifice at the feet of Jesus. When she fell to the floor before Him, she didn't open the bottle and carefully measure out the droplets of perfume. She broke the bottle! She doused His feet with the costly essence. Mary ignored the criticisms and grumbling aimed her direction. All she saw was the Lover of her soul.

What an illustration of unrestrained worship—genuine and complete praise and worship. No perfunctory prayers. No half-hearted communication because it's expected of us. No sideways glances at those who might disapprove of our actions. God yearns for us to worship Him with Mary's intensity of devotion.

The Shulamite bride is the one for whom the Bridegroom will return. This is the radiant woman of Revelation, clad in a glowing garment of praise and thanksgiving—the robe of Christ's righteousness, woven especially for her on the loom of Calvary. Better yet, our honeymoon with God will never end. The ongoing revelation of God's nature only increases our hunger to know and love Him more.

The psalmist declared:

> Whom have I in heaven but you?
>   And earth has nothing I desire besides you.
> My flesh and my heart may fail,
>   but God is the strength of my heart and my portion
>   forever. . . .
> It is good to be near God.
>   I have made the Sovereign LORD my refuge
>   (Psalm 73:25, 26, 28).

In *The Message* paraphrase, Eugene Petersen renders the verses this way:

> You're all I want in heaven!
> You're all I want on earth!
> When my skin sags and my bones get brittle,
> Yahweh is rock-firm and faithful. . . .
> I'm in the very presence of God—
> oh, how refreshing it is!
> I've made Lord Yahweh my home.

A poet said, "Home is the place where, when you have to go there, they have to take you in." For many people that isn't true. But with

God, my Beloved, it is always true! Can you think of a better place to call home than the one filled with an unconditional love that will grow throughout all eternity?

GRACE NOTES

- Close your eyes. Take a deep breath. In that one breath, you inhaled 150,000,000 molecules of air. At least one of those molecules, Jesus breathed when He was on the earth. How awesome to breathe the same air as the Savior breathed. Thank God for the air He keeps perfectly balanced for your consumption.
- Look at a scar on your body. Remember how you acquired it and the pain you felt. Like a little child, show it to Father God. Read the promise of healing found in Psalm 103:1-3. Thank Him for healing you in His chosen time.
- Stand before a full-length mirror while you read aloud Psalm 139:13, 14.
- Construct a Möbius band as described in the text. Before taping the ends together, write the following words on the strip, "God's infinite love for [insert your name] has no end." Hang the Möbius band next to your bathroom mirror to remind yourself, every morning and evening, of God's infinite love for you.
- Find examples of the five senses—smell, touch, sight, hearing, and taste—used in the Song of Solomon. Read them aloud as declarations of love to your spiritual Husband. Create a few of your own declarations of love to share with God.

SECURE IN THE ESSENCE OF HIS PRESENCE

Take your everyday, ordinary life—your sleeping, eating, going-to-work, and walking-around life—and place it before God as an offering. . . . Fix your attention on God. You'll be changed from the inside out
(Romans 12:2, 3, *The Message*).

"Where were you when . . .?"

Each generation has a tragic, defining moment to remember. For my great-grandparents, it was the first Battle of Bull Run. For my grand-parents, it was the sinking of the *Lusitania.* For my parents, it was the Japanese attack on Pearl Harbor. For me, it was the assassination of John F. Kennedy. For my daughters, it was 9/11. "How could such a thing happen?" was the response, regardless of the year it occurred. The tragedy that will define my grandchildren's generation—I shudder to think what it might be.

Like many other Americans, for me the lingering aftermath of the 9/11 tragedy has been a required dose of CNN each morning to be certain that the world beyond my doorstep is still intact. Once I am assured that society's same old problems are the same old problems, I can proceed with my daily tasks. Grief counselors might consider this to be a symptom of post-traumatic stress or perhaps a cry for comfort. Perhaps it's both.

Massive calamities hold a horrific fascination for humans. Such monumental events have a way of becoming all-consuming. During a tragedy it is difficult to remember what life was like before the disaster and that there will be a life following. And the more devastating the event, the more absorbing it is. That's what sells news and Lincoln SUVs.

Pursuing God can be forgotten in the glare of life's "virtual reality." I can forget that my true reality is found in the divine world; virtual reality is so often the focus of the life I live on planet Earth. Only as I focus on my Creator do the events surrounding my life, good, bad, or tragic, fall into a proper perspective. Worship takes me out of my circumstances to a place where I can view life, even horrific happenings, with a "God's eye view." It takes me to a place where I can balance my temporary discomforts against the Savior's promise of eternal joys. Time with God in the morning can give me a glimpse of the larger perspective, and I am better prepared to face the problems of the day, whether found on the television or in my parlor.

The apostle Paul wrote about the joy of living in the essence of God's presence:

> I know what it is to be in need, and I know what it is to have plenty. I have learned the secret of being content in any and every situation, whether well fed or hungry, whether living in plenty or in want. I can do everything through him who gives me strength (Philippians 4:12, 13).

The Message paraphrase puts it like this:

> I'm glad in God, far happier than you would ever guess. . . . Actually, I don't have a sense of needing anything personally. I've learned by now to be quite content whatever my circumstances. I'm just as happy with little as with much, with much

as with little. I've found the recipe for being happy whether full or hungry, hands full or hands empty. Whatever I have, wherever I am, I can make it through anything in the One who makes me who I am.

What is the essence of God's presence? First, consider what the essence is not. We've all met people who seem to have bathed in cologne. They wear enough fragrance to make one's eyes water even when standing clear across the room. (Being allergic to many perfumes, I've been known to move to another area of the church in order to escape particularly pungent cologne.)

As a teenager, I went through a perfume-dousing stage, an after-bath splash. With help from long-suffering family members and friends, I quickly learned that a dab or two of perfume was all I needed to surround myself with the essence of my favorite perfume.

Unfortunately "wannabe" Christians wear their religion like cheap cologne. I call them "wannabes" because an in-your-face religion is not Christianity (see Philippians 4:4-8). Their own particular brand of musk accosts all those they meet—in waves, ad nauseam. God's essence always draws (and never repels) others toward Him. Like a quality perfume properly applied, the essence of God's presence in one's life comes across as a whisper, not as a scream.

On her fortieth birthday, Sandi* found herself traded in by her husband "for two twenties," as the not-so-funny joke goes. Her struggle to raise three elementary-age children alone was anything but funny. Trying to juggle the needs of three children and holding down two full-time jobs to make massive house payments sapped her strength and her health.

Sandi had never wanted to be an independent woman. To go it alone became more and more unthinkable. Late at night when the children were sleeping, her thoughts turned toward suicide as the solution. If she could be brave enough to end it all—ah, sleep in total peace—her

---

*Not her real name.

children would be better off without her. She knew she could count on her parents to raise her babies. In her twisted, pain-filled mind, Sandi believed suicide was the most loving gesture she could do for everyone. Satan had turned her world inside out and upside down. He had done the same with her thinking.

This is a favorite ploy of the father of lies—to convince his victim that suicide is an acceptable means of getting out of everyone's way, a genuinely unselfish act of love. Sandi reasoned that a self-inflicted demise would be her final gesture of compassion for her family.

This idea is common among depressed individuals. This isn't self-pity; it's twisted logic. "I'm depressed and I make everyone around me depressed. If I weren't here they could get on with their lives."

Why should we be surprised? The devil sees death as his ultimate triumph. But what he blocks from the discouraged individual's memory is that Christ's sacrifice on the cross broke the bonds of death forever. Hallelujah! God the Father has better plans for His children, "plans to give hope and peace."

One night as a winter snowstorm pelted Sandi's home, the woman decided she could not face another day. With a bottle of sleeping pills in one hand and a bottle of alcohol in the other, she went to the phone to ask her mother to come over and watch the children for a few hours. She would ingest the cocktail of poison when she hung up the phone. By the time her mother arrived, it would be too late.

Instead of getting a dial tone, Sandi heard someone singing on the line, "Jesus loves me, this I know; / for the Bible tells me so."

Impossible, she thought. *I have a private line.* Thinking the anomaly might be due to the storm in the area, she hung up the receiver. A minute or two later she returned to the phone.

Again she heard a little child singing, "Jesus loves me this I know . . ."

Sandi waited ten minutes and tried again to place her call. ". . . Little ones to Him belong; they are weak, but He is strong. Yes, Jesus loves me . . ." When the truth of the child's simple words broke through her frazzled brain, she hung up the receiver, dumped the booze down the sink, and returned the sleeping pills to the medicine chest.

The phenomenon continued for many days. Whenever she tried to place a call, she heard, "Yes, Jesus loves me . . ."

This quirky little miracle triggered Sandi's desire to get reacquainted with the God who loved her so much He'd rather die than live without her. Her slow, step-by-step journey took her beyond a mere moment with God each morning and evening. She knew her very survival depended on her diving into this God-thing heart first.

When she stumbled across Jeremiah 3:14, the passage in which God promises to be her husband, Sandi thought, *All right! I am going to romance God in the same manner I would if He were courting me.* She tidied up her hair-do, spruced up her wardrobe, and restyled her mental outlook. These changes alone improved her daily attitude. Another change she made was to think of Scripture as a love letter from her Intended—instead of a prescription drug to take twice a day.

Her worship, both at church and at home, improved. Whenever she found herself in her Lover's presence, she purposely blotted out everything and everybody except Him. Before long her expression became radiant. Like a bride standing at the altar, face to face with her beloved, Sandi glowed from the inside out. She didn't need five layers of Cover Girl™ to mimic good health and youthful vigor. She'd fallen in love with her new Husband and, in doing so, discovered the secret of living in a fabulously new environment—in the essence of His presence. Did all of her difficulties disappear overnight? Of course not! But with confidence in her new Spouse, she knew they could see through the difficulties together.

Sandi's story became more meaningful to me one afternoon, thanks to my grandson. My daughter and I were chatting while her two young sons played quietly by our feet until three-year-old Jarod found a picture of his favorite animal, a "snakey." Immediately he wanted me to share in his joy.

"Grandma, look!" He tugged on my sleeve.

"Yes, Honey." Involved in my adult conversation, I brushed him off with a nod and a pat on the head. The toddler saw my response for what it was—disinterest.

"Grandma! See!"

Again I pretended interest for an instant and then returned to his mother's and my conversation. Frustrated, Jarod took my face between his two hands and drew my face close to his. Staring eye to eye, the serious little boy tapped his hand vertically on his nose and said, "Grandma! Focus!"

This was the attention-getting technique Jarod's father, a former academy choir director, used during rehearsals and performances. It was also the way Mark redirected his young son's attention when necessary.

"Grandma! Focus!" Jarod had something vitally important to show his grandma and he wanted my undivided attention. Anything less would not do.

The need to focus is not only necessary for good communication, but it is the key to breaking through to the presence of God. Have you ever felt God tugging on your sleeve, saying, "Focus, Honey, focus"? For years, what I had called worship could better be described as a "fast food" experience at church or a prayer and Bible text "snack" every morning and evening. Until I readjusted my focus, I didn't know what I'd been missing.

God calls His people to a higher level of worship than I once could have imagined. True worship is so much more. It focuses on God and God alone. The best gift you can give the Father is your attentiveness. That's what Scripture calls, "worshiping in spirit and truth."

The Master Teacher said to the woman of Sychar, "An hour is coming, and now is, when the true worshipers shall worship the Father in spirit and truth; for such people the Father seeks to be His worshipers. God is spirit, and those who worship Him must worship in spirit and truth" (John 4:22-24, NASB). True worship is all about God, not about us.

When I began my new worship adventure, focusing on Him alone became a battle of the mind and the will. Too often my prayers sounded like, "Dear Father, I come before You to worship You—*am I scheduled to have special music this Sabbath or next?*—as my Lord and King. Thank You for—*maybe I should invite the Nelsons over for Sabbath dinner this week. We owe them big time. No, the living room carpet is too dirty*—You are my Creator, my Savior—*Did Jarod remember to turn off the spigot after playing under the hose this morning?*—Lord, I love You and worship You . . ." And so it went. I sometimes felt when I tried to pray that I was surrounded by screaming voices, snatching my attention from the Father and blotting out His quiet, gentle voice.

As a budding musician, my younger daughter Kelli wished she could go to bed one night and wake up an accomplished pianist. It never happened. She learned that developing "musical muscle" takes practice—like it or not. Climbing Mt. Everest takes years of rigorous training, not from a casual fifteen minutes here or there, but a determined focus on the goal to make it up the mountain. Even a fledgling baker must practice adding just enough flour to her dough to make a decent pie crust. If she's distracted by the TV or with chasing toddlers, she'll lose her focus and her results will be compromised.

Learning to focus on God takes practice too. A college science professor gave each of his students a simple object to study and then instructed them to write up their findings. At the end of the class period the students handed in their observations. The next day the professor handed them the same object; he told them to study it and then compose a new list of observations. Each day for a week the assignment was the same. Just as the students thought they couldn't discover one more new thing about the object, they found something else. The professor was teaching his students not only to look at but to actually see the object before them.

Focusing on God is similar. Looking in His direction and reciting His attributes is only the beginning to truly "seeing" Him. The more we focus on Him, the more we discover about Him and His character. In Revelation, we're told that the task of the highest order of angels is to circle the throne twenty-four hours a day and sing hallelujahs to God. I thought that was a difficult feat until a pastor friend improved my perspective. He suggested, "Viewing a prism from different angles gives you new colors to appreciate and a new perspective on the same object. Likewise, hallelujahs naturally burst forth from the chosen angels as they, with each turn, discover new and exciting 'colors' of the Infinite One."

Focusing our attention and energies on God increases our capacity to enjoy a deeper, richer, more intimate experience with Him. As we enthrone Him front and center in our thinking; as we view His multi-faceted beauty; as we glorify His name in the privacy of our personal retreat or while standing in the congregation, it becomes easier and easier to remain focused on Him.

A synonym for *focus* might be *consecration.* In *My Utmost for His Highest,* Oswald Chambers writes, "Consecration is our part; sanctification is His part; and we have to deliberately determine to be interested only in that in which God is interested."[1]

My grandson Jarod was wise enough to know that he couldn't share the excitement he felt upon discovering the picture of his favorite "snakey" with me, until he had my exclusive attention. Likewise, if my attention flits here and there, I can't experience the excitement God the Father feels about the miracles He wants to perform in my life. He needs my undivided attention in order for me to appreciate the changes He has in store for my heart.

Jesus Himself gave us the example of an intimate, one-on-one worship with the Divine. While large crowds clamored for His attention, Christ often slipped away in the night to commune with His Father. He needed the quiet time of rest and rejuvenation. Intimacy with the One who loved and understood Him better than anyone else meant more to the Master than casting out demons, healing lepers, or raising people from the dead.

Upon returning from their mission trip, the Savior instructed His disciples to "come with me by yourselves to a quiet place and get some rest" (Mark 6:31). Today's disciples need to put aside life's demands and the expectations of others and slip into His presence each day. This is not optional to our love relationship with the Eternal God; it's crucial.

If we neglect to come apart and worship the Father, we will not bear lasting fruit. Our Christian experience will exist in the realm of urgency and crises, instead of in a constant arena of peace and joy. Our ministry to family, friends, and co-workers will be stunted. And we will experience the torture of knowing Him only from a distance. Worse yet, we will never realize what we've been missing.

Taking time to experience an intimacy with God makes stony hearts tender. That was what Martha needed. She had a busy ministry entertaining the Master, but it was Mary who knew Jesus. Some Bible scholars point to Mary as the one disciple who understood the Savior's mission. We do know that she loved Him with her whole heart, and nothing would deter her from expressing her love.

Whether we've been believers for six months or sixty years, we can fall in love with Him over and over again by sitting at His feet the way Mary did and absorbing His goodness.

When I fix my eyes on Jesus, He will return the gaze. As I embrace His presence, He will speak to me. He will call me by name. "Kay, you are so beautiful to Me." Can you hear Him calling you? Insert your own name; the message is the same.

"I am love. Whoever lives in love lives in Me, and I in him" (see 1 John 4:16). The strength of your life rises or falls with your willingness to spend time alone with the Savior. The choice to pursue God is yours, not your mother's or your father's; not your aunt's, uncle's, or pastor's—but yours alone.

GRACE NOTES

- Record on paper or cassette tape your memories of one defining moment in your life. Include your emotional reactions to the event. What biblical promises helped you grow beyond the crisis?
- Recall a time when a child in your life taught you a valuable truth about God. Share it with someone.
- Try on "something old." Perhaps it is a musical instrument you played as a child, a recipe you used to enjoy making, or a favorite retreat you haven't visited for some time. Go back and savor those memories. Lift your praises to God for the often unsung gift of memory.
- Close your eyes. Picture Jesus walking on a sandy beach along side the Sea of Galilee. Describe the look of joy that comes on His face when He sees you running toward Him. Experience the emotions you would have when He scoops you into His strong, bronzed arms. In simple, childlike terms, tell Him how much you love Him.

TO THE HEART OF WORSHIP

I will sing of your love and justice;
To you, O LORD, I will sing praise
(Psalm 101:1).

I am a child of old-time camp meetings where the music stirred the spirit and revitalized the soul. "Redeemed how I love to proclaim it! / Redeemed by the blood of the Lamb!" "What a fellowship, what a joy divine, / Leaning on the Everlasting Arms." "To God be the glory, great things He hath done." After such a song service, the worshipers were ready to be fed.

It was at a camp meeting in Union Springs, New York, that I, as a ten-year-old, first gave my heart to Jesus Christ. I can still smell the sawdust and hear the tent ropes groan as the wind off Lake Cayuga whipped the heavy canvas above our heads. Elder H.M.S. Richards, Sr., made an altar call that evening and, while I was certain the call was meant for adults and not kids, the Holy Spirit tugged at my heart. I knew I had to go forward.

What did Elder Richards preach about? I don't remember. What songs did we sing? I don't remember. Who had special music? I'm not sure. But I am sure that my decision, made in a moment of sincere worship, saw me through the tough teenage years that would follow. Yet as beautiful as my memory of that service might be, it isn't enough to sustain a relationship with my Lord.

Sincere worship must be more than a fond memory or a once-a-year camp meeting high. I need a spiritual anointing today, every day. Everything I do should be acts of praise and worship to my King, whether singing praise choruses in the congregation, making dinner for the family, swimming laps in a pool, or riding a dirt bike over a bumpy mountain path. Hymn writer Fanny Crosby expressed this concept beautifully in "Blessed Assurance." "This is my story, this is my song, / Praising my Savior all the day long." Worshiping Jesus Christ is fundamental to living the Christian life. Hebrews 12:2 advises, "Let us fix our eyes on Jesus."

Living in the essence of His presence takes a passion for the relationship; it takes my commitment. To describe this heightened level of personal commitment, I have only one experience with which to compare it—Richard's and my marriage. It's been an ongoing love affair for forty years. When I travel solo across the continent, the essence of Richard's love goes with me. I am content knowing he loves me. I feel safe knowing he is praying for me. Whether I am speaking to large audiences or small, a reference to my beloved always seems to sneak into my presentations. I don't always plan for it to happen; it just does. You see, I am married to an incredible guy, and I can't keep it to myself. It's not bragging; it's a fact— and I have a tendency to tell what makes me happy.

Other reminders of the essence of Richard's love are Post-it notes. That's right, Post-it notes tucked into my suitcase, amidst my undergarments and in the folds of my bathrobe, in my program notes and my Bible, wrapped around my shampoo bottle, stuffed in the toe of a shoe. These messages—sometimes gushy, sometimes silly, always personal— declare his undying love for me.

I leave behind similar notes for him to find. He's likely to run across my notes in his briefcase, in his underwear drawer, in his Bible, in his jacket pocket, on his computer screen, on the refrigerator door, on the TV screen. And with the arrival of the Internet, I have an e-card sent to him, one a day for however many days I'll be out of town. The personalized greeting cards make coming home to an empty house each evening a little more pleasant for him.

Whether in Georgia or Hawaii, Alaska or Massachusetts, I call him on the phone each evening. We chat about a little bit of everything and a whole lot of nothing. We share the latest happenings and news of our days, the weather, and occasionally the day's political events. He has to tell me about the latest Doonsbury® cartoon, and I have to repeat the newest joke I've heard. Just hearing his voice refreshes me. Our phone conversations always end with "I love you" and "Drive carefully." "Drive carefully" is just another way to say, "I love you. Take care of yourself."

Phoning Richard is never an obligation. As exhausted as I might feel when I return to my room at the end of the day, I never think, "Oh, bother! I've got to call Richard. Tsk! I'd better get it over with." Quite the contrary, no matter how tired I am, when I hear his voice at the other end of the line, I am rejuvenated. If I close my eyes, I can almost feel his arms around me. I could talk with him all night—if we could afford the phone bill.

And his little love notes aren't just a stack of scrap to be read and then discarded. When I see his "1-4-3" scrawl in heavy, bold print, my heart soars. Yet as eager as I may be to receive our daily ten-minute phone calls, the emotion pales before the anticipation I feel as my plane circles Fresno Yosemite International Airport for a landing on Sunday night. My heart rate goes up; my smile broadens as I paste my face to the aircraft's window. I know that in ten minutes or less, I'll be in his arms. All the phone calls, all the quirky notes cannot equal seeing him face to face and hearing him say, "Welcome home, Darling!"

In my love affair with Jesus, the communication I receive through letters (Scripture) and phone calls (prayer) will never equal the intensity of emotion I'll experience when, one day, I see Him face to face and I hear Him whisper, "Kay, I missed you so much! Welcome home." But until that day, just as Richard's notes and phone calls sustain our love while we're apart, God's love letters and our daily worship time together must do the same.

Our worship time together? *Together?* Is that a typo? I thought I was the one doing the worshiping. True worship is interactive—worship time together; for true worship is never a spectator sport. *Interactive* is a "pitch word" for our generation, used to describe everything from the newest Ninetendo™ game to calling in your vote for your favorite musician on a TV talent show. However, the concept is not really new. God's children have been experiencing interactive worship since the beginning of time.

When I come to Him with a monologue, blurting out my requests, whining about my burdens, and giving Him no opportunity to respond, I am not worshiping. I may be praying, but I am not worshiping. My worship becomes interactive when I pour out my heart to my heavenly Bridegroom. In response, He moves the deep recesses of my being, the place referred to in Psalm 139. My senses come alive to His presence. I thrill at the sound of His voice; I thrill at the touch of His hand. I thrill at the sight of His countenance. I am deeply moved by His presence. Herein lies the heart of worship, the key to living in the essence of His presence.

The word *worship* comes from two Greek words, *pros* and *kuneo*. The word *pros* means "to move forward." The word *kuneo* means to "kiss with a sense of awe." Earnest worship involves both a physical action and a loving intent. That's why no one can praise Him exactly like I can. My praise is as uniquely mine as my fingerprints, my eye prints, and my tongue print.

God isn't listening for the perfectly sung worship chorus but for the simple expression of Kay's heart. Just as I grew teary-eyed at the scrawl, "I LuV U, MomEE," on my daughters' first hand-made Mother's Day cards, so God treasures my unique, uneven attempts to voice my love for Him. And when it's not there, the Father misses it.

Zephaniah 3:14-17 gives a beautiful picture of God's side of interactive worship. So much of the Bible is male orientated. This passage is distinctly feminine. Instead of women adjusting to being called "sons of God," the men in the congregation must adjust to being called "daughters of Zion." (A little sensitivity training is good for the soul.)

First, imagine God seated on His throne. Is the chair overlaid in gold? Or is it an upholstered, velvet reclining sofa? Perhaps you see a plush, upholstered leather desk chair behind a massive mahogany desk, similar to the one in the President's Oval Office? Location! Location!

Location—wise counsel from your real estate agent, but with God, location doesn't mean a thing.

When you prepare to worship God, He's not on His throne as much as He is with you, whether you are lounging on your sofa or kneeling beside your bed. The place where you find yourself is unimportant. When you begin to rejoice, God leaves His environment to join your environment. True, the Holy Spirit is the One who enters your world, but name or title doesn't matter—it's still all God. The members of the Trinity are One. God the Father isn't sending a lesser god to your side. And when you worship, you have His undivided attention. How does He do it? I haven't the slightest idea. To me, it's mysteries like this that make Him God. Perhaps in the kingdom, He'll answer our questions regarding His omnipresence. And then again, perhaps this one will remain His little secret.

Verse 14 begins with my part in the interactive worship. "Sing, O Daughter of Zion"—that includes me! "Shout aloud, O Israel!" When was the last time you shouted aloud the words "I love You, Jesus"? The idea came alive to me at a Washington camp meeting a few years ago. I was there to tell stories to the Primary age children. It was those six- to nine-year-olds who taught me how to rejoice. Remember, it was Jesus who said, "Truly I say to you, whoever does not receive the kingdom of God like a child shall not enter it" (Mark 10:15, NASB).

The meeting tents for the various age children were in a giant circle separated by lawns and walkways. Rain or sunshine, the children were so eager to attend their meetings that they gathered outside the fences at their particular tent until the directors opened the gates. Their eagerness to worship God was impressive, but that's not what moved me.

As the children waited, they began singing a chant. First the juniors would sing, "I love Jesus; yes, I do. / I love Jesus, how about you?" Then the Primary children, from across the oval, would answer and direct their chant toward the group of teens outside their pavilion. The teens would reply and aim their question at the kindergarteners. Round and around the groups would sing, each trying to out sing and out shout the others.

"I love Jesus; yes, I do. / I love Jesus, how about you?" Can you imagine an adult service beginning with that kind of enthusiasm?

"Be glad and rejoice with all your heart, O Daughter of Jerusalem!" What would happen if we grown-ups rejoiced with all of our hearts? Just what would happen?

Verse 15 says, "The LORD has taken away your punishment, he has turned back your enemy." To know that my sins are forgiven; my justifiably deserved punishments suspended, gives me incredible joy. And who is a greater enemy to me than me? I'm my own worst enemy. There are times I don't like myself very much at all. My mouth gets me into jams (and not strawberry!) of my own making more often than I care to admit. And not only my words! With a lift of an eyebrow or a knowing nod, I can belittle a sister or a brother. God's promise to turn back my enemy makes me want to rejoice even louder than before.

"The LORD, the King of Israel, is with you; never again will you fear any harm." Wow! Imagine never being afraid of the future again?

On Easter Sunday several years ago, my family and I stood in the pre-dawn darkness of the Grand Canyon. With a stiff wind out of the northwest and frigid spring temperatures, we huddled together beneath a heavy woolen blanket. We'd come to the national park for a break from the pressures of a major crisis for our family. We would be moving, but where we did not know. Frightened and fretful, Richard and I didn't know where to turn, so we retreated from the battlefield.

After a short reading by a local pastor, a soprano began singing the first verse of Bill Gaither's familiar hymn "Because He Lives." As the first words of the chorus filled the early morning air, the sun crept above the eastern horizon as if on cue. We watched in awe as darts of light skittered along the rocky crags, filling one canyon after the other with sunshine. By the end of the third verse, the entire canyon was illuminated with sunlight and warmth.

What blessed assurance we found that morning. Tears rolled down our faces. We hugged one another. We could face our tomorrows because of Jesus' sacrifice. We worshiped a living Savior, not a god whose body lay in a distant marble tomb. We could face whatever troubles might come our way because the God who saved us did so out of an infinite love for us. And He promised, "Lo, I am with you always, even unto the end of the earth."

That worshipful moment has stuck with me through all kinds of trials and tribulations. A great cause for rejoicing, don't you think? Notice that the above verse in Zephania doesn't say, "You will never again experience disaster in your life." It says my fear is gone. In this marvelous relationship with my Beloved, a personal trouble becomes an opportunity for joy! (See James 1:2.) I'm not saying I always look at a toothache or an editor's rejection slip as an opportunity for joy, but I have the promise that, should I choose to keep my love with God growing, I will one day reach that point. My troubles will become challenges and testimonies to His glorious name.

Like any great love between two individuals, growing is a step-by-step, day-by-day process. Verse 17 says, " 'The LORD your God is with you.' " I like this better than the translation found in the Life Applications Bible, which is "living among you." "Living among you" sounds as if I have to share Him with the neighborhood. I don't. Call me selfish, but my personal worship with my Beloved is exclusively mine to experience. I need to feel His presence. I need to inhale His essence. I need to taste and see that the Lord is good; I need to savor the heady flavor of His love.

"He is mighty to save." In Hebrew the word *mighty* can mean noble or honorable—"He is honorable to save." It can mean He is strong enough to save. The synonym I like for *mighty* is *eager*. He is "eager to save." For many years I lived with the misconception that there was a big chalkboard in the sky, and beside my name I'd earned an unending row of check marks. Every check mark had to be erased or I'd miss recess (i.e. heaven and eternity).

Another illustration I once had of my relationship with God is of the donkey and the carrot. I was the donkey and heaven was the carrot. A capricious god was holding a carrot just beyond my reach to keep me struggling toward my destination.

As I've become better acquainted my Beloved, I've discovered that both views are faulty. God wants to save me, not condemn me. He doesn't want to lure me into heaven with the promise of carrots or even golden streets. There is a joke about a greedy man, who, due to a computer glitch, accidentally slipped through the Pearly Gates. Discovering that heaven's highways were paved with pure gold, his avarice got the best of him. The man sneaked off to an isolated corner of the kingdom. There he began chopping away at the roadway. He was so busy gathering his exciting new treasure he didn't hear two angels approaching.

"What is that man doing?" The first angel asked.

"I don't know." The second angel shook his head in disbelief. "What in all the universe does the poor guy want with chunks of pavement?"

When living with the King of the universe, gold is reduced in value to macadam, tar, and so much cement. For me, whether heaven's thoroughfare is paved with gravel, macadam, or gold is immaterial as long as it leads me straight to His arms.

John 15:9 describes God's love like this. " 'I've loved you the way my Father has loved me. Make yourselves at home in my love' " *(The Message)*.

Someone once said, "Home is where the heart is." During our forty years of marriage, Richard and I have lived in houses of brick and adobe; stucco and clapboard; houses with aluminum siding and houses badly in need of a paint job. Our very first home, a duplex in Loma Linda, California, was plaster sprayed over chicken wire. I discovered the fact the hard way one day when I was changing around our bedroom. I poked a corner of the bed frame through the plaster. From then on we stuffed the hole with tissue to keep out any vermin that might be wandering in the neighborhood. But one fact is certain, over the years, regardless of the quality of our living quarters, Richard's presence made each house a home for me.

Home means being able to sit down to the dinner table without waiting for an invitation. Home allows me to kick off my shoes and curl up on the sofa. Home is where I can shed my stuffy business duds and slip into my purple house dress. So what if the garment is permanently stained with acrylic paints or the fabric is "pilly" with age; I'm at home. I am home where I am loved, not because of my speaking ability or lack thereof; not because of my winsome smile or lack thereof; not because of my wit, intellect, or loquacity, or again, lack thereof. I can take a deep breath and exhale because I'm finally home.

Back to God's being eager to save. When I think of the term *eager,* I remember Richard's adventure mushing in Alaska. One of the dogs on the team had run in the Iditarod. These creatures live to run. While he was climbing on board the sled, the dogs danced and wriggled about impatiently. When given the signal to go, they leaped down the trail. Those puppies were eager to run!

Likewise God is eager to save. The God of the universe eagerly awaits my signal to take over my life. He's eager to help me, eager to comfort me, eager to work out my problems according to His pre-ordained plan.

"He will take great delight in you." I am a woman who takes great delight in her family. When either of my daughters says, "Mom, how would you like to go bonding?" (i.e. shopping, rent a video, attend a concert), I drop what I'm doing and go. I love being with them.

The same is true when I anticipate being with Richard at the end of the day. While I've never been considered a stunning, fair-haired beauty, fifteen minutes before his arrival, I rush to the mirror to spruce up my limp, English locks. I take a few moments to pat a touch of color onto my cheeks. Now I don't do this because I have to. He loves me when my hair droops like limp celery leaves; he loves me when my complexion resembles a peeled onion—but I take delight in him. I am eager to please him. I'm eager to be with him, and I want to give Him my best.

If God takes great delight in me, what does that mean? Tuesday and Thursday afternoons are "grandma days." I pick up my younger grandson from daycare. When I park my car in the driveway, two-year-old Alec is already peering out of the floor window next to the front door. He's bouncing up and down, saying, "Gamma, Gamma, Gamma!" When I open the front door of the house, he throws himself into my arms. I immediately begin loving him with kisses and hugs. Once we're situated in the car—and that's a task in itself with child seats, seat belts, backpacks, "binks," bottles, and "blankies"— I back out of the driveway onto the street and begin to sing a very special love song that goes like this:

Gammy, Gammy, Gammy, Gammy loves you;
Gammy, Gammy, Gammy, Gammy loves you;
Gammy, Gammy, Gammy, Gammy loves you;
Yes, I do; yes, I do; yes, I do! Do! Do!

Alec always joins me on the last "Yes, I do" with an additional "do, do, do" of his own. The simple song will never make the nation's top-ten song charts, but it brings incredible delight to the heart of one very special two-year-old and to his equally enamored grandma.

God takes great delight in me when I accidentally brush my teeth with Cortaid™, one "tingly" toothpaste! He delights in me when I praise Him to a friend. He delights in me when I sing Hallelujah instead of fuss when I miss a green light. He delights in me when I traipse through a college campus with my skirt accidentally tucked in my pantyhose, or when I try to boil an egg in a microwave—not a good idea. Instead of scolding me for being so hapless, I can hear Him laugh and say to Gabriel, "Look! That's my girl." I am His girl, no matter what the circumstance. That's what God's delight is all about.

I pause when I read the part of the verse 17 in Zephania chapter 3 that says, " 'He will quiet you with his love.' " When our younger daughter Kelli was a small child, she loved to climb into her daddy's lap at the end of the day. "Scratch, daddy, scratch," she would say, meaning she wanted a backrub. She would snuggle down into his lap while he rubbed her back.

One night, many years later, Richard and I received the dreaded, middle-of-the-night phone call that stops the strongest of parents' hearts. There'd been a serious car accident. And while Kelli was physically safe, her best friend had been killed in the crash.

We immediately drove the four hours to where Kelli and her sister had been visiting. Richard and I were exhausted by the time we arrived. But we had one thought, and one thought only, *Were both girls safe?* They were shaken but somehow holding together. When we asked if they wanted to sleep a few hours before returning home, in unison, they both agreed they couldn't sleep. They just wanted to go home.

Our older daughter Rhonda, hyper-tense from the events of the night, asked if she could drive home. It was decided that I would sit in the front to keep her awake while Richard and Kelli rode in the back seat. Now Richard never sits in the back seat of the car. This time he did so without a word of protest. Shaken by the evening's events, Kelli curled up in her father's lap and whispered, "Scratch, daddy, scratch."

Later Richard would tell me that the strong odor of motor fuel and bits of gravel in her hair reminded him of how close we'd come to losing our precious baby girl. The purr of the engine and the gentle, familiar touch of her father's hand lulled our stressed-out daughter into a dreamless slumber throughout the entire four-hour drive home. No longer a little child, our sixteen-year-old feared she wouldn't be able to sleep after the night's tragedy, but Richard's love had quieted her. "He will quiet you with his love."

I've heard people say, "I can't hear God. I feel so alone. When I pray, He's not here for me." Wait, could it be that He is holding you in His arms and trying to quiet you with His love? Could the Father's silence be evidence of the closeness of His presence instead of His distance from you? Could it be that His love for you is so great that mere words fail to express His emotion for you, much like they did my husband as he held Kelli in his arms? Could it be that you and I are complaining about our situation so loudly that we miss hearing His still, small voice and sensing His very real presence? Didn't He promise, "I will never leave you nor forsake you"?

My favorite phrase in Zephaniah 3:17 is, " 'He will rejoice over you with singing.' " That word *rejoice* has nothing to do with joy, a continual state of well-being—an attitude for living. *Samah,* the Hebrew word for rejoicing, refers to a spontaneous emotion or extreme happiness, the kind that arises at festivals and weddings, or at the overthrow of one's enemies. In today's terms, it is the roar of the crowd as the winning ball drops into the basket an instant before the buzzer sounds.

Samah is a feeling so strong that it must find expression in some external act. This is the word used to describe King David dancing before the sacred altar or the cheering women celebrating his victorious return from war.[1]

Historians say that *Samah* means total abandonment of proper protocol to the celebration of the moment, kind of like the emotional response I expect to have when I first see Jesus coming in the clouds.

The first edition of the Good News Bible paraphrased the phrase another way. "What is that singing I hear? Is it a choir? No, it is God singing over His children."

What part do you imagine Him singing? Base? Tenor? Baritone? Perhaps He sings four or five choral parts all at once. Why not thirty-five? Or seventy-six? What a celebration it must be for the angels each time the Creator of sound and harmony breaks forth into singing over you. Over me! Kind of makes me want to echo His praises back to Him.

But the best example of Zephaniah's interactive worship is found in verses 19 and 20. " 'I will give them praise and honor.' " Imagine God praising you and honoring you, instead of the other way around? Some-how it's easier for me to praise God and glorify His name than it is for me to imagine the Creator praising and glorifying me.

And then Zephaniah says, " 'I will bring you home.' " This is the moment all Christians are waiting for—going home.

A song writer of the 1970s touched the hearts of believers every-where when he wrote, "Welcome Home, Children." Instead of writing from the human perspective, he wrote the lyrics from God's perspec-tive. "Welcome home, children." What a climax to the ultimate inter-active worship experience, hearing our Father say, "Welcome home." I plan to love Him forever. How about you?

GRACE NOTES

- Record on paper or cassette tape your memories of the day you first gave your heart to God.
- Sing or listen to the lyrics of a love song from your youth, one containing words that can apply to your relationship with God.
- Recall the emotions that sprang out of your first love or your first kiss. Record the memory in your praise journal.
- Write a sonnet to your Beloved, or if you're not a poet, complete the simple, four-lined poem, "Roses are red, violets are blue . . ." Place a copy of your love poetry in your Bible for future reference.

RECIPES FOR WORSHIP

The Lord says, "These people come near to me with their mouth and honor me with their lips, but their hearts are far from me. Their worship of me is made up only of rules taught by men"
(Isaiah 29:13).

Nothing tastes better on a crisp autumn evening than a bowl of homemade lentil soup. And it's so simple to make. Here's my recipe:

1 lb. Uncooked, washed lentils
1 Minced onion
1 c. Chopped celery
3 Large tomatoes, diced
2 Cloves garlic, minced
1 Bunch of spinach, chopped
  Salt to taste

Place the lentils, onion, celery, tomatoes, garlic, and spinach in a crock pot 3/4 full of water. Cook on high for 2 to 4 hours, and then simmer until dinnertime. M-m-m-m! It's simple to make and is guaranteed to "warm the cockles of your heart."

A great recipe for interactive worship is equally as simple and satisfying:

> Take one generous serving of praise
> A bunch of thanksgiving
> One or two confessions, as needed (sincere and specific)
> A desire for the Holy Spirit's presence
> A dash of music that glorifies the name of Jesus (optional)
> One well-worn Bible (for variety, use other translations and
>   paraphrases)

Place all of the above ingredients in an open heart, stir in a helping of joy, and then, simmer quietly until the aroma permeates your entire being. Then you will savor the flavor of a great personal worship.

You might have your own recipe for lentil soup and for your personal worship. You might add rice to the pot for a thicker soup. You might add hot sauce for extra zip. You might throw in a handful of chick peas. That's fine when we're talking about lentil soup—but can you alter our culturally refined recipe for worshiping God? Never! There's one correct way of worshiping, isn't there?

If you want to grow as a Christian, here are the seven tried-and-true steps you must follow to worship—with no variations: First, plan for a thirty- to sixty-minute quiet time, morning and evening. Second, read one to three chapters a day from God's Word. Third, pray the Lord's Prayer twice a day, three times on Sabbath. Fourth, sing all five verses of "A Mighty Fortress." Fifth, faithfully attend church every week, no exceptions allowed. Sixth, be involved in every program sponsored by your church. Seventh—OK, so I'm being silly. Thank God there is no such recipe for worship.

Too often we approach our personal worship the way we would a daily dose of canned, generic-brand soup. Good stuff. I've eaten my share over the years. I ate it as a kid. My mom used to eat canned soup as well.

So did my grandmother. A little bland perhaps; a tad boring day after day, not very nourishing, but it was good enough for my ancestors; it must be good enough for me! If someone suggests adding a pinch of dill or a dollop of chili sauce to boost the flavor, I might look askance at his audacity. How can they suggest that I in any way alter my old standby? And should someone else suggest that I make a pot of lentil soup from scratch using fresh ingredients, I'm likely to say, "No thank you! I am perfectly comfortable with my simple, generic, easy-to-prepare soup."

You might protest, "You don't know what you're missing."

And I would reply, "That may be true, but I don't care. I feel safe eating my trusty canned lentil soup. Any other recipe just wouldn't taste the same. And who knows what might be in it—regardless of the list of ingredients on the can?"

Such an attitude toward canned soup is laughable; the same attitude toward worship is sad, especially when we impose our generic, all-inclusive methods of worship on the people around us. "It's my soup or no soup; it's my way of worship or no worship!"

Worship nourishes the soul in the same way food nourishes the body. If you've ever been frustrated with your quiet times with God, hold on. If you've grown bored sitting at a desk reading; if you've felt imprisoned by a rigid formula; if your inherited recipe for worship is no longer feeding your soul, I've got good news for you! It's all right to vary your spiritual diet.

Why should a computer programmer in California's Silicon Valley worship God in exactly the same way as a Cape Cod fisherman? Why should the mother of five preschoolers struggle to squeeze into the same worship pattern as her professional nine-to-five counterpart? We don't expect people to dress exactly alike, shop in the same stores, or go to bed and get up at the same time. Why should worship be forced into one tight-fitting worship box?

True communion with God frees, not inhibits, the worshiper. "Worship, at its best, flows as sweetly as milk and honey, and is as nourishing," author Kathleen Norris wrote in *Amazing Grace: A Vocabulary of Faith.*[1]

When we expect others to live life exactly as we live it, whether it be worship or eating lentil soup, we remove the very gift Jesus came to give to His disciples—freedom. Christ hated the oppressive rituals that the organized religion of His day had imposed.

Jesus came to break the bonds of pomp, ritual, and culturally accepted behavior. He touched the leper; He included Mary, a fallen woman, in His circle of disciples; He stared down demons. He spent His time talking to little children. Even when Jesus told the disciples to distribute the fish and the barley loaves to the assembly, He was breaking social barriers. Serving food to the crowd was servant's work or woman's work—both of which was beneath a Jewish man. Jesus came to free men and women from iron chains of their own making. He wanted to show His beloved disciples that freedom came when serving another.

Speaking to the woman at the well, Jesus said that one day His people would worship Him in spirit and truth. This concept of worshiping God was totally different from the cultural religion of His day. Too often worshiping in spirit and truth is still diametrically opposed to our own culturally limited thinking.

When Jesus was walking the streets of Jerusalem or trudging the highways of Galilee, He met the needs of each person differently. It was He who created the individual with a unique personality and spiritual temperament. How He must revel in our sometimes clumsy, sometimes humorous attempts to say, "I love You."

God implanted in His children a spiritual hunger that may be satisfied in different ways—just like lentil soup. My daughter Rhonda dislikes lentil soup, homemade or otherwise. I enjoy it. She'd prefer her grandmother's Pasta e Fagioli. (Actually, I wouldn't mind a bowl of that myself.) Our personal time with God becomes more satisfying when we worship in the way that is natural and comfortable to us.

Obviously there are scriptural limits to an individualized approach to worship. In the story of Cain and Abel, Cain thought he could worship his own way. When God asked for a lamb offering, Cain chose to give Him fruit. God directed the first brothers to sacrifice sheep for a reason. He wanted to point them toward the Crucifixion. Fruit couldn't do that. It would take the shedding of blood to complete the purpose of the Cross. This particular form of worship was fulfilled at Calvary.

While we, as Christians, view Christ's sacrifice after the fact, we still have guidelines laid down in the Word. The apostle Paul makes it quite clear that a person's expression of faith must occasionally be joined to the corporate worship found within the body of Christ. God set aside the Sabbath for that purpose. Our Creator knew we would need one another in order to develop into healthy and productive Christians. Three of the many avenues God uses to speak to us are the Word of God, the world of nature, and the experiences of our fellow believers. No one is so intellectually strong or spiritually mature that he or she can't learn more about the Father from his sisters or brothers in Christ.

And then, of course, there is the threat of false worship. On PBS television or on the pages of *National Geographic,* we've seen examples of demonic worship practiced by primitive tribes in exotic places like New Guinea or the Amazon Basin. Whether their sacrifices include dangling upside down from a cross or cutting themselves with knives, the Creator of heaven and earth is not the god being honored. Can you imagine our Creator taking pleasure in watching His creatures maim and mutilate themselves?

But we don't need to travel to remote jungles for a view of false worship. A visit to Stonehenge, England, on June 21st, the summer solstice, is far enough. Each year on the longest day, 25,000 or more people pay homage to the religion of the Druids. Any Friday night in Santa Cruz, California, you can find professed Satanists worshiping their god on the beach along West Cliff Drive.

Don't be deceived. God is not slow to condemn false worship. The first and second commandments prohibit worshiping strange gods: " 'You shall have no other gods before me,' " and, "You shall not make for yourself an idol' " (Exodus 20:3, 4).

Other Old Testament passages make it clear, for example, that child sacrifices are abhorrent to Him and not a legitimate way of showing love to the Creator. In Amos 5:21 God says, "I hate, I despise your religious feasts; I cannot stand your assemblies." What is God speaking about here? Were His people worshiping false gods? God goes on to say, "Even though you bring me burnt offerings and grain offerings, I will not accept them. Though you bring choice fellowship offerings, I will have no regard for them. Away with the noise of your songs! I will not listen to the music of your harps." What were these people doing that God would abhor their worship? Verse 26 answers that question. "You have lifted up the shrine of your king, the pedestal of your idols, the star of your god—which you made for yourselves."

"God hates worship by the people who go through the motions only for show. If we are living sinful lives and using religious rituals and traditions to make ourselves look good, God will despise our worship and not accept what we offer. When you worship at church are you more concerned about your image or your attitude toward God?"[2]

How important it is that we worship God in a way pleasing to Him. When I married my husband, I knew he detested lemon meringue pie. He'd mentioned it many times during our courtship. In our forty years of marriage, I've never made him a lemon meringue pie—not ever. If I'm going to expend time and energy to make him a special treat, I would choose to make him an apple pie or a peach pie, not one he abhors. So it is with God. Since worship is all about God and not about me, I want my worship to be pleasing to Him.

In the book *Sacred Pathways: Discover Your Soul's Path to God,* Gary Thomas identifies a variety of worship styles displayed in the Bible:

> Scripture tells us that the same God is present from Genesis through Revelation even though different people worshipped that one God in many ways. Abraham . . . built altars everywhere he went. Elijah and Moses revealed an activist streak in their . . . conversations with God. David demonstrated an enthusiastic, celebratory type of worship, while his son Solomon, expressed his love for God by offering generous sacrifices. Ezekiel and John described loud and colorful images of God, stunning

in sensuous beauty. Mordecai demonstrated his love . . . by caring for others, beginning with the orphaned Esther. Mary is the classic contemplative, sitting at Jesus' feet. John the Baptist gives glimpses of what we might call the ascetic [worshiper].[3]

The nine styles of worship discussed in Gary Thomas's book are not meant to trap the individual into a rigid pattern, but to free him. Knowing and understanding the variety of paths available can help the worshiper better understand himself and his brothers and sisters in Christ. There may be good reasons why one worshiper best experiences the Holy Spirit's presence amidst the majesty and splendor of high-church while his brother prefers communing with the Spirit while walking in a grove of California redwoods.

The Naturalist. The Naturalist receives the greatest blessing worshiping God in nature. When out of doors, his heart soars to the Creator. He finds spiritual refreshing while studying the stars or watching ants scurry in and out of an anthill. He draws closer to his Creator when surrounded by the things God made. His theme song might be, "I Sing the Mighty Power of God" or "How Great Thou Art."

The Sensate. The Sensate worshiper loves God with her senses. She wants to be lost in the awe, beauty, and splendor of God. She is drawn to the liturgical, the majestic, and the grand. Intricate architecture, classical music, and formal language send her heart soaring. The five senses are the most effective inroads to her heart. Hearing Saint-Saens' Organ Symphony Op.78 will bring her to tears as quickly the fifty-fifth time as it did the first time she heard it.

The Traditionalist. The Traditionalist loves God through ritual and symbol. Regular church attendance, tithing, responsive readings, and Sabbath keeping feed his worshiping spirit. Experiencing the same ritual week after week creates a greater depth and texture to his Christian faith. The traditionalist comes alive when studying the symbols found in the Old Testament sanctuary or the beasts described in the book of Daniel. He prefers singing songs like "O God, Our Help in Ages Past" to the newest praise chorus.

The Ascetic. The Ascetic wants nothing more than to be left alone in prayer. He best experiences the presence of God in total solitude minus all the frills. Take away the liturgy, the trappings of religion and the noise from the outside world, and he's happy. Even when worshiping in a group, the ascetic often isolates himself from the others. As to his music preference, he enjoys listening to the "music of the spheres"— total silence.

The Activist. An Activist serves a God of justice. He relishes the account of Jesus cleansing the temple. He defines worship as standing against evil, "though the heavens fall," and calling sinners to repentance. Church is a place to go to recharge the batteries for waging war against injustice. He is revitalized by confrontation. "Onward Christian Soldiers" or "Stand Up, Stand Up for Jesus" would be the sound of his battle cry.

The Caregiver. The Caregiver loves God best by loving others. She sees Christ in the poor and downtrodden. Her faith is built around serving others. Remember Peter's mother? After being healed by Jesus, she didn't fall down to worship at His feet. She arose and immediately served her guests. A good example of this temperament would be Mother Teresa. On the streets of Calcutta she saw a need and set out to fill it. She is quoted as saying, "It's not enough to say you love God. You also have to say you love your neighbor." "Into a Tent Where a Gypsy Boy Lay" moves a caregiver to tears.[4]

The Enthusiast. The Enthusiast loves God through mystery and celebration. The word *enthuse* comes from two Greek root words: *en* meaning "in," and *theos* meaning "God." Where a sensate wants to be surrounded by beauty and the intellectual prefers to grapple with concepts, the enthusiast is inspired by joyful celebration. This is God's cheerleader. She doesn't just want to know spiritual concepts, she wants to touch them, to feel them, to hear them, to be moved by them. She has a childlike trust in God's mysterious power to work out everything according to His will. The Enthusiast would respond to hymns such as "Redeemed! How I Love to Proclaim It" and "The Joy of the Lord Is My Strength."

The Contemplative. The Contemplative loves God through contemplation. She refers to God as a loving Father and the Bridegroom. Her favorite passages might come from Song of Solomon. Her focus is not necessarily serving God and doing His will as much as loving Him with the purest, deepest, brightest love imaginable. Mary worshiping at Jesus' feet would be a kindred spirit to the contemplative Christian. "My Jesus, I Love Thee" and "As the Deer" would speak to this worshipper.

The Intellectual. The Intellectual loves God with his mind. Primarily he lives in a world of concepts. This Christian will be studying issues such as the ordination of women, predestination, the work of angels verses the Holy Spirit's job description, or the state of the dead. Faith is something to be understood, more than experienced. He feels closest to God when he uncovers something new about Him. "Be Thou My Vision" might be his prayer.[5]

As you review the nine pathways to worship, you probably found yourself comfortable with more than one type. That's good. The complete Christian will display many, if not all, the spiritual temperaments. King David certainly could be described as a spiritual "Renaissance man" for his day. Perhaps that's one reason he is described as "a man after God's own heart." David sought his Lord in every way possible.

Four essential elements in every true expression of worship are loving God with all our heart (adoration), soul (will), mind, (belief), and strength (body). The intellectual is not excused from adoring God. Nor is the beloved excused from harboring wrong beliefs about God. By understanding our spiritual temperaments, we can develop the tools we need to grow spiritually. However, we must keep in mind that God initiates and sustains our relationship with Him. The study of these temperaments merely helps the worshiper better understand the spirit God gave him.[6]

Worshiping God is a way of life, with many facets of expression. By becoming aware of possible worship patterns, we can enhance our own experience with God. Also we can better appreciate our brother's or sister's worship choices without condemnation should they differ from ours. Most important, the Lord enjoys the diversity of sincere worship when expressed through His Spirit and in truth.

To stress the importance of personal worship, Pastor Thomas uses the illustration of two gardeners. One tends to her vegetable garden regularly while the other walks away once the seeds are in the ground. At harvest time, the first woman is thrilled with the abundance while the second discovers that her vegetables have been raided by birds and overgrown with weeds. She seriously questions the value of gardening. The secret of the first woman's success was in the tending.[7]

If you think that your spiritual garden only needs an initial planting to flourish, you are mistaken. To become a mature Christian takes daily tending to the soul. Whether your worship times need a little weeding here or there or a major cultivation, understanding your spiritual temperaments can improve the bounty of your devotional harvest.

GRACE NOTES

- Make a pot of your favorite stew. As you prepare the food, give thanks for the benefits your body will receive from each ingredient.
- Analyze your daily worship pattern. What is working for you? Why? What isn't it working? List ways you can add variety and spice to your worship time with God.
- Try out a fresh worship pattern today. Perhaps you can take a walk in the woods, listen to Handel's *Messiah* on your stereo, or sit on the floor beside Mary and listen in silence to the voice of God speaking to your heart. Record your responses and impressions in your praise journal.
- Find examples from the life of Christ that illustrate the nine pathways He took in His worship.

THE ELEMENTS OF EFFECTIVE WORSHIP

Applause, everyone. Bravo, bravissimo!
Shout God-songs at the top of your lungs!
(Psalm 47:1, *The Message*).

I love to sing! As a teenager I dreamed of becoming a Broadway star. My favorite television program was *Your Hit Parade*. In the week following each episode, I would hang my mother's sheets on our pulley clothesline for stage curtains and act out the numbers in my backyard. (And they say TV doesn't affect kids!) Eventually, common sense, fear, and the lack of adequate talent prevailed. I went to college instead, became a teacher, married my lovely Italiano, and birthed two beautiful daughters. Good choice!

I know what it is to sing and to refrain from singing. For two years of my life I couldn't squeak out a note; once, before I was healed of asthma and again, following major surgery. I hated being silent. God intended for this kid to be a show-off for Him. Silence wasn't part of my worship style. It hurt not being able to worship in my usual way. Yet during each of my years of silence, God increased my capacity for worshiping Him in other ways. Digging deeper in His Word for understanding increased my spiritual agility. Silent time alone with Him taught me to be still and know—to know, not just think, He is God.

Despite differing personalities and spiritual preferences, all worship will be enhanced by the inclusion of these elements: praise, gratitude, requests, confession, scripture, and a time for reflection. However, not every spiritual encounter with God includes every element. For instance, it's unwise to read the Bible while driving on a freeway at seventy miles per hour, but I can lift my voice in praise. And it is socially unacceptable to sing praise to Him while sitting in a physician's waiting room. Yet I can use the long wait to "be still and know."

I like to begin my planned worships with praise. Sometimes I sing my praise; other times, I laugh, I dance, or I whisper love poems I've composed for Him. Overcome by His majesty and power, I've been known to fall on my face before Him. Sometimes I wrap His love about me like a two-year-old might hug his favorite "blankie." At that time my praise might be accompanied by sniffles or moaning, but it is still a defiant praise. "Yet I will rejoice in the LORD," as Habakkuk wrote (Habakkuk 3:18, KJV).

Praise is a choice a child of God makes every moment of every day. Praise differs from thanksgiving because it is an action I choose to take, regardless of my circumstances. I praise God for who He is and thank Him for what He's done. That's a huge difference. Wives, thanking your husbands for remembering to take out the garbage is just good manners, but reminding him that you love him for his faithfulness to you is praise. Husbands, thanking your wives for making a great apple pie is courteous; but telling her that you treasure her more than diamonds, that's praise.

King David gave us a beautiful example of praise in Psalm 104:1. "O LORD my God, you are very great; you are clothed with splendor and majesty." That's praise, not for His creative prowess or His generous gifts of love, but for who and what He is.

Praise is similar to human love. I choose to love my husband even when he acts unlovable. I might not like him at the moment, but I choose to love him. And he does the same for me. (Yes, I admit it. I can be quite unlovable at times.) This act has nothing to do with my feelings for him, and everything to do with the vows we made to one another many years ago. And so I praise God because of the vows I made to Him. Even when I am tempted to whine, fuss, or question His goodness, I choose to praise Him.

Praise is a part of worship because it is the language of heaven and earth. Beings on far-distant planets, angels circling His throne, all creation praises God (see Psalm 148). The sun, the moon, the stars praise God. The creatures of the ocean depth sing their Creator's praises. I have a CD recording of Orca whales singing to one another. Scientists have studied the beasts and are convinced that the animals are doing more than communicating emotions, warnings, or directions toward a food source. There are definite patterns to their songs.

All of nature praises God with no hidden agenda, no wish list—the purest of praise. Lightning darting across a midnight sky, lazy snowflakes falling on a wintry morning, majestic mountains soaring into the clouds—all praise God. Palm fronds swaying in the trade winds, aspen leaves fluttering in the golden sunlight, sea gulls swooping and soaring above the surf, lambs cavorting in the meadows, seals clapping their flippers following a hearty meal—how God treasures His creatures' sincere praise!

Despite all this adulation, it's your praise and mine that He most desires. The slowest of created beings to praise, humankind has the most about which to praise. We alone can understand "sonship" and "daughtership" with the King of the universe. We alone comprehend the adoption plan formulated before the creation of the world and consummated at Calvary. We alone can grasp the implications of God's sacrifice, His forgiveness, and our eternal inheritance. We alone know how unworthy we are. Do squirrels scampering up and down tree trunks in the park grasp the wickedness of their sins? Do dragonflies darting about the garden understand the profound implication of the Cross? Do bobcats in the forest appreciate God's promise of eternity?

Without praise, our worship takes on a mere "form of godliness," as described in 2 Timothy 3:5, "having a form of godliness but denying its power." Such a person is the most dangerous of religionists—all heat and no heart—the breeding ground for fanaticism.

Have you ever heard someone say, "I wish I had more faith"? Guess what? They have all the faith they need if they choose to praise. What these people really want isn't more faith, but a stronger faith. And having a stronger faith is up to them. God planted a seed of faith in every human heart. And He's given 8,000 promises for us to claim to help that seed to grow.

Wishing for greater faith is like longing for the ability to pump 100 pounds of iron without doing the work to build the necessary muscles. Praise is to faith what exercise is to the muscles of the body. Wishing won't do it. Believe me, I've tried. Just as my leg muscles strengthen through exercise, so my faith muscles grow stronger by praising.

I admit it. It's not natural to praise while facing financial reversals. It's not natural to praise at the graveside of a loved one. It's not natural to praise following the physician's pronouncement that you have cancer. It's not natural—but it's godly.

Staring down major adversity by faith becomes easier if our daily workout includes praise. Our praise—turning our thoughts to God—has been building strength through the minor difficulties day by day. The faithful mentioned in Hebrews 11 didn't reach the pinnacle of faithfulness without first exercising their faith through everyday experiences. When we praise Him despite our hardships, we are confirming to the universe that we belong to Him and that we believe that His promises are true. When we gripe, complain, or whine, we are saying to all creation, "I doubt God is who He says He is and that He means what He says."

Praise is our identification badge to the universe. Americans have learned how important one's proof of identification is when traveling. After dropping my driver's license twice in the Atlanta airport in the weeks following 9/11, I carry my ID in a plastic pocket on an elastic cord around my neck. Shopkeepers, ticket agents, and security guards can instantly see that I am who I say I am.

That's also how praise works. When I open my mouth to praise, everyone knows I belong to my Dad, who gave His children this identity: "You are a chosen people, a royal priesthood, a holy nation, a people belonging to God, that you may declare the praises of him who called you out of darkness into his wonderful light" (1 Peter 2:9).

I've discovered that praising before complaining eliminates the complaining. How can you whine to God after you've praised Him for His wisdom and power? Before you know it, the bigger trials that used to spin your life out of control become easier to face.

I can attest to this faith-building exercise firsthand. As a Christian speaker, I've stumbled upon (or over) an interesting phenomenon. Two weeks before speaking at a major weekend retreat, I've often found myself in a turmoil regarding my health, our finances, or an emotional relationship—my personal bugaboos. These distractions would destroy my concentration, making it difficult to spiritually prepare for the upcoming weekend. These attacks were as regular as a sunshiny day in California's San Joaquin Valley. When I discovered that other Christian speakers experience a similarly distressing time prior to their engagements, I realized these attacks came, not by chance but by design from the father of lies. By stealing our joyful anticipation of the event, he could make us weak (see Nehemiah 8:10).

Now with my eyes open to Satan's wily attacks, I can fortify my faith muscles ahead of time. So I can laugh and shout in his face, "Too bad, you old devil! Your worn-out bag of tricks won't throw me this time. In the name of Jesus, leave me alone!"

Worship without praise produces spiritual boredom. If you have trouble reading Scripture or staying awake during your evening time with God, try starting your worship with praise.

The beauty of praise as a faith-building exercise is that I can work out anywhere, in any weather, at any time. Swimming laps is boring in and of itself, but it has become one of my richest praise times. After three or four round trips in the pool, I lose count of how many laps I still need to swim to meet my goal. My inability to remember has helped me turn my physical exercise into a spiritual mid-morning snack from God's buffet table.

This is what I do. During my first three laps, I concentrate on the Trinity. While I praise the Father, I picture myself walking hand in hand with Him; Jesus, my Brother , is swimming by my side, stroke by stroke; and I praise the Spirit for the awakening of senses as I glide through the water. Next, I assign a lap to each person on my prayer list. While on each lap, I pray a prayer of affirmation. I resist the urge to correct all the bad in the person's life. I let God do that. Instead, I ask the Creator to design a special blessing of peace, joy, or love especially for that individual. Before I know it, I've completed my affirmation list—and my physical exercise for the day. This quirky style of worship works for me. I have a friend who uses a similar routine when she walks or jogs. Instead of laps, she uses the intervals between telephone poles for each subject.

The second ingredient that enhances one's worship is gratitude. "Give thanks in all circumstances, for this is God's will for you in Christ Jesus" (1 Thessalonians 5:18).

Wow! Do you want to know God's will for your life? Begin by giving thanks in all things. After you've taken the first step—giving thanks—He will add another, and another. Step by step, God will show you the way.

How can I give thanks for all things? Some tragedies are beyond thanksgiving. Does God expect me to lie? A Christian woman splayed on a restroom floor with her attacker hovering over her cannot be expected to give thanks for being raped and beaten, can she? A good question, one with which I wrestled for many years until I reanalyzed the verse.

Little things make a difference, a comma here, a question mark there. Look closely at the preposition in that command. The verse says, "Give thanks *in* all circumstances," not "*for* all circumstances." What a difference the word *in* makes. While I can't honestly give thanks for all things, I can give thanks in all things because God is with me in all things. Whether I'm facing down a drugged-out rapist or a dialysis machine, I can know God is with me, and I can give Him thanks for that. I can know God will see me through this crisis. The psalmist reminds me that my Shepherd walks with me through the "valley of the shadow of death" (Psalm 23:4). I'm not alone—ever! Therefore I can give thanks in all things, because God keeps His word. Hallelujah! That should set your vocal chords to praising.

A grateful heart is one of the characteristics of citizens of God's kingdom, the kingdom where you moved when God adopted you into His family. Unfortunately, giving thanks is neglected by many Christians. In Romans, God was angry with certain individuals because they did not acknowledge the God of heaven and were ungrateful (see Romans 1:21).

But, Kay, you may ask, isn't it natural to complain when things go bad? Aren't we supposed to take our burdens to God? Of course! It's not the sharing of our troubles with Him that causes us problems; it's the interfering with His perfect plan, as if we know better what is best for us. As the Lord spoke to the prophet Isaiah, "My thoughts are not your thoughts, neither are your ways my ways" (Isaiah 55:8). God's way of thinking is far beyond our ability to grasp. That's why the Holy Spirit has been commissioned to reveal to us the heart of God (see 1 Corinthians 2:10).

Another problem of bringing our troubles to the worship altar is we don't often leave them there. We spread our petitions out before the Father with great eloquence, say Amen, and then stuff them back into our pockets for future reference. Later, we take them out and examine them to see if God has done anything about them yet. We're a bit like a kid picking the scab off his knee to see if his wound is getting better. Praise and gratitude allow us to leave our burdens in God's hands and move on, knowing He said He'd take care of them—and He always keeps His promises.

Giving thanks in all things is neither a denial mechanism nor an attempt to escape from reality (see James 1:2). Giving thanks in all things gives us a "God's eye view" of our world. We no longer have only our self-centered point of view. This change in perspective gives us a fresh, new paradigm by which to live—God's paradigm.

You can determine to dwell in an attitude of gratitude. The simple solution has nothing to do with gritting your teeth. Before He returned to heaven, Jesus promised that the Holy Spirit would help us whenever we ask. Even the nastiest habit can be broken through the Holy Spirit's power. If you ask the Holy Spirit to warn you before you fall back into the sins of grousing, griping, judging, or fretting, He will. Then you can make a conscious choice on whether you wish to resist or give in to the old temptation.

GRACE NOTES

- Read Psalm 103. Line by line, claim it as your personal psalm. Ask the Holy Spirit to remind you as to how God has already answered this prayer in your life. Thank Him for those victories. And then, read the psalm again, projecting the promises into your future and thanking Him for those victories as well.
- Make the choice to praise. Place notes of praise psalms all over your house as reminders.
- Write a note of praise to a former teacher, a family member, or a friend. Thank him or her for the positive impact that person's Christian example made on your life.
- Create a super-sized Thank-You card to God and post it beside your bathroom mirror. Read it every morning and evening.

MORE THAN A CHORUS LINE

Let us fix our eyes on Jesus
(Hebrews 12:2).

"All together now! It is time to worship our God." And all the voices blend in a rousing round of "Ha-la-le-la-la-le-lu-la-le-lu-jah! Ha-la-le-la-la-le-la-le-lu-jah!"

Praise and worship is more than a chorus line, more than skillfully blending harmonies or singing an intricate obbligato to someone else's melody line. Great precision, such as a line of Rockettes performing on the Radio City Music Hall stage, doesn't necessarily produce a successful corporate worship atmosphere.

True worship is about more than singing a line in a hymn. "O worship the King, ta-da-da-da-da ..." You've sung the song so many times before; you could sing it in your sleep. If this is true, then you might as well sing it in your sleep for all the worship experience you will have. No matter how lovely the sacred lyrics, if sung without thought, it is just noise to God.

Worshiping our Savior is fundamental to living a faith-filled, Spirit-led Christian life. Unfortunately, many Christians have no idea what it means to worship God.

George Barna, president of Barna Research Group, reports, "Worship is among the highest priorities of God. Each weekend millions come to church but few understand. Two thirds of regular churchgoers cannot describe what worship means. Our research shows that a majority of those who attend worship services in any given week (more than three-fourths of all adults) do not experiences the presence of God during worship. In fact, half of all churchgoers admit that they have not felt connected to God or in His presence at any time in the past year, in spite of their regular attendance at church. Even so, only 4 percent of senior pastors in Protestant churches list facilitating or enhancing worship as a top priority. Those who do indicate that the energy is being put into determining the best music, the appropriate forms of technology and how to pack out the worship center."[1]

Some worship leaders claim that a certain defining style of worship is the only correct way to worship. Fortunately, we don't have to be great singers or musicians to worship God, just extravagant worshipers like Mary as she poured out her expensive perfume on Jesus' feet.

Extravagant worship involves the giving of ourselves totally to Him. Extravagant worship is a genuine movement in our hearts, thoughts, and wills toward God's heart, thoughts, and will. Throughout the Word, whenever one of God's children demonstrated extravagant worship, God responded with extravagant blessing. Noah was an extravagant worshiper. He'd just witnessed the drowning of all humankind, except him and his immediate family. Yet, the first thing Noah did when he left the ark was to offer a sacrifice of praise (see Genesis 8:20, 21). When the Lord smelled the pleasing aroma of Noah's sacrifice, He gave the covenant promise that He would never again destroy all living creatures with a flood. Noah's extravagant worship came in obedience to God.

Abraham built an altar on Mt. Moriah. He intended to sacrifice his son Isaac. He was prepared to give God the thing he loved most—that's an extravagant worshiper. David prayed for an "undivided heart" (see Psalm 86:11).

Mary emptied a bottle of perfume over Jesus' feet. She wasn't stingy; she didn't measure it out drop by drop. She held nothing back. And the aroma of her lavishly extravagant worship permeated the banquet room and filled all of heaven.

In a filthy prison cell two extravagant worshipers sang praises to God despite the chains on their ankles and wrists and the open wounds on their bodies. Their music was heard beyond the prison walls, over the buildings of the city, above the stratosphere, directly to the throne of God (see Acts 16:23-29).

Worship, love, and obedience are inseparable. Can you imagine God seated on His throne, leaning forward to better hear the praises of His two faithful sons, Paul and Silas? And then His foot begins tapping on His footstool—the earth is God's footstool (see Isaiah 66:1), and He set the jailhouse and everyone in it rocking! Paul and Silas's extravagant worship led to God's extravagant rescue and one of the most beautiful conversion stories ever recorded.

Extravagant worship is like extravagant love. Can I really worship God extravagantly? That sounds like a mighty big order to fill. After all, I know myself. I was never voted the "most likely to succeed" in anything. I never won any gold medals or a popularity poll; I have never been a woman of exquisite beauty; I never earned superior grades in school; and no teacher ever predicted great things from me, though one or two predicted the opposite. So I know that anything I do is a testimony to God's grace alone.

Many people battle with insecurity. However, union with Christ in worship is not a matter of emotions. It is not something we are to feel but something we choose to do. When drawn into worship by a deep abiding love for the Author of love, the inferiority issue will fade. We can lift up our heads in worship, not because we are self-confident, but because we are God-confident. We can stand proud, not for anything we've done but because we are adopted daughters and sons of the heavenly King. We have been created for a divine purpose. We were created to worship the Father (see Hebrews 10:19-23). Our Father says to us, "I don't care about your talents; I don't care about your musical ability. I don't care about your great looks or lack of them. All I want is you. All I want is your undivided heart."

The other day I was working with two-year-old Alec on his obedience issue. After a short timeout, I reminded him about the importance of obeying me. To ensure that he got the point, I asked him, "Honey, now what are you going to do the next time Gammy says, 'Obey'?"

The little boy thought for a moment, then looked soulfully into my eyes, and said, "I don't know." Ah, the honesty of children. Alas, it pains me to say that my children and my grandchildren are not perfect from a human perspective. They make mistakes. Knowing that fact in my mind and seeing with my heart are two different things. To me they are totally beautiful, the most perfect gifts God has ever given me. Only a parent can understand. Whenever my daughters ran to my arms or planted sticky candy-coated kisses on my cheek or scribbled "I Luv U" on a homemade Mother's Day card, I wasn't concerned with any of the naughty things they might have done previously. I never said, "Be careful, you're going to wrinkle my dress" or "Wash your hands and face. You'll mess up my makeup" or "Honey, you misspelled 'I love you.'" At that moment they are perfect.

In the story of the prodigal son, when the boy ran to his father's arms, the dad didn't see his son's matted hair; he didn't smell the stench of his body. All he saw as his beloved son—he had come home.

So it is with my heavenly Parent. Whenever I worship, my Father is exalted. My insecurities, my pesky problems, my bad habits, even my feeble attempts at trying to be good shrivel to unimportance. When I worship, God looks past the ugly, the good, and the tawdry found on my less-than-stellar record. He looks straight to my heart. When I worship Him extravagantly, He frees my mind and His of all other thoughts. When we worship together, He basks in my demonstration of love, and I freely soak in His presence and am overwhelmed by His grace.

"When people come together to worship, they come exactly as God knows them, with their differences, their wildly various experiences and perspectives. And by some miracle, they sing, and listen, and pray as one. In [corporate] worship, disparate people seek a unity far greater than the sum of themselves."[2]

If I ask the Holy Spirit, He will teach me how to worship. He will anoint my mind for worship. He will touch the depths of my innermost being. He wants to awaken in me the ability to lose myself in worship. He delights in a people who delight in Him. I pour out my love on Him, and He pours out His love on me. It works both ways.

"We praise God not to celebrate our own faith, but to give thanks for the faith God has in us. To let ourselves look at God and let God look back at us, and to laugh and sing and be delighted because God has called us His own."[3]

GRACE NOTES

- Practice praising someone, perhaps a son, a daughter, a spouse, or a parent, for who he is instead of what he or she did or can do for you.
- Read Psalm 148 in the King James Version of the Bible. Read it again in a newer version. Let your mind expand to the edges of the universe—"All creation praises God."
- List your personal bugaboos—you know, the buttons Satan knows to push that will upset your spiritual peace. Read the list aloud and, in the name of Jesus, laugh in the devil's face. Then praise God for the knowledge you now have to defeat your greatest enemy—yourself.
- Consider the term *extravagant worship*. How can your worships become more extravagant and less ritualistic?

PICKING
UP THE PIECES

Ascribe to the LORD the glory due his name.
Bring an offering and come before him;
worship the LORD in the splendor of his holiness
(1 Chronicles 16:29).

Nothing is as precious as a child's first prayer.

One evening Kelli and Mark were helping their son Jarod with his evening prayers. First Kelli would say a line—"Dear Jesus . . ."

And then Jarod would repeat, "Dear Jesus . . ."

"Thank You for this day . . ."

"Thank You for this day . . ." And so on.

But on this evening the two-and-a-half-year-old boy decided he was big enough to pray his own prayer without parental help. It went something like this: "Dear Jesus, thank You for this day. Thank You for ice cream. Thank You for . . ." and his list was endless. Just as Kelli suspected his prayer might be a new stalling tactic, Jarod moved on in his prayer. "Bless Mommy and Daddy; bless Grandma and Grandpa Rizzo; bless Grandma and Grandpa Wheeler; bless Uncle Randy, Aunt Rhonda, and Uncle Tracy. Bless all the jet pilots and," he paused for a moment before ending his prayer with, "and help Mommy and Daddy to obey me. Amen."

Was his prayer merely a take off on the usual ending to his parents' evening prayer, "Help me to obey Mommy and Daddy"? Or did the little boy know exactly what he was praying? Probably we'll never know. By the time the child is old enough to tell, he will have forgotten.

For many years I prayed prayers similar to Jarod's—"Dear Jesus, help God to obey me!" Have you ever prayed such a prayer? Perhaps your prayer was less strident than, "My way is the only way; now do it!" But the message was still the same. Most of us have. When worships are limited to whimsical requests and childish demands, our relationship with Him can't mature past the "gimme" stage of childhood.

We really are the children of God, and the dynamics of our relationship with Him are more similar to the relationship between earthly parents and their children than we might initially believe. Since earthly parents don't have the same attributes and capacities to love as does God, we struggle with this. We know our own limitations as moms and dads, and we project those limitations onto our heavenly Father.

Providing for your child isn't a burden but a pleasure. My daughter Kelli didn't understand how much enjoyment I took buying things for her and her sister until she became a mother. Now when she goes shopping, she finds greater delight buying things for her two boys than buying for herself. God Himself set the example. Jesus said, " 'It is more blessed to give than to receive' " (Acts 20:35, NKJV). He, even more than earthly parents, seeks to enjoy this blessing called happiness.

Wise parents do not respond immediately to every whim but sometimes test the desire level in their children. One week it's, "Daddy, can I have a Jimmy Neutron™ action figure?" Next week it's, "Daddy, can I have a Nemo™ toy?"

As children mature, parents might require them to save their own money to buy their latest desire. Working for a new bike or video game, for instance, will add value to the object in the children's eyes. So it is with God and His children (see Luke 11:13).

Other times a parent waits for the child to ask. "You do not have, because you do not ask God" (James 4:2). God loves hearing our prayer requests. He wants us to ask Him to fulfill the desires of our hearts, not so He can test us, but so we can learn by testing Him. Prayer is a conversation that matters both in heaven and on earth. Jesus said, "Ask and you will receive, and your joy will be complete" (John 16:24).

Sometimes God is a permissive parent (see Luke 18:1-8). He listens to us and genuinely responds to us (see Joshua 10:14). When my grandson Jarod asks me to take him to the local dollar store after school on Thursdays, I will sometimes tease him by saying, "We'll see." He's not content with a "We'll see" answer.

"Grandma, tell me," he'll say.

And I will reply with another "We'll see." All the while we banter over whether or not to go to the dollar store, I am driving in the direction of the store. Our little game ends when Jarod pauses to look around and sees where we are—at the dollar store. Did I change my plans? No. Did he change my mind, affect my decision? Was I a permissive grandparent? No, my plans hadn't changed. I knew where I was going all along. Likewise, God knows the end from the beginning. He is our "never-changing Father." From our perspective, we sometimes think we have prevailed over God's *permissive* will. He allows us that victory in order to better understand His *perfect* will for us.

I used to enjoy wrestling on the living room floor with my dad. Of course I didn't stand a chance of pinning down a father who could lift 200-pound scaffolding onto his shoulders and carry it from his truck to the next job site. Before we began, he knew the outcome of our contest. He didn't wrestle to prove his strength against his eight-year-old daughter's. We tussled in the carpet in order to bond. Our wrestling also increased my strength and agility.

God and I wrestle in prayer for the same reasons—to bond and to develop my spiritual strength and agility. A Christian athlete once pointed out to me that wrestling is the only sport in which the opponents never break contact. I like that. When God and I wrestle through a problem or a situation, He will never break contact with me. No matter how far

I go, His love will still be there for me. I may have some apologizing to do, but He won't let go of me. That's reassuring.

While God knows when, where, and how best to answer our prayers of request, our prayers of penitence are always and immediately answered with a Yes. He assures us of His forgiveness: "If we confess our sins, he is faithful and just to forgive us our sins, and to cleanse us from all unrighteousness" (1 John 1:9, KJV). This is a truth made possible at Calvary.

Jim, a veteran of the Vietnam War, was meeting with his pastor. More than anything else, the soldier wanted to believe the man of God when he said, "God will forgive your sins." But Jim just couldn't believe.

"Pastor," he said, "you don't know how bad I've been."

To which the minister replied, "You're right; I don't, but God does. And He forgives you regardless."

"When I was in Vietnam, I did something terrible. . . ." The man covered his face with his hands. When he looked up, his eyes were filled with pain and self-hate. "One day, after a fire fight where all my buddies were mowed down by the enemy, I broke rank and ran into the jungle. Out of my mind with grief, I came upon a small bamboo chapel. Several old men, women, and small children were singing 'Shall We Gather at the River.' Pumped with adrenalin, grief, and fury, I opened fire on the worshipers, killing them all. Do your really believe God can forgive me for that?"

The pastor took a deep breath before he spoke. "Jim, if God can't forgive you for killing those people, He can't forgive me for my sins either. For forgiveness to be real, it must work for everyone; it must cover every sin."

When Jim failed to respond, the pastor continued. "If you don't believe God can forgive your sins, either you are saying that your standards are higher than God's or that the Savior's sacrifice on the cross wasn't good enough.

"Forgiveness is all about Him, not about you. In Old Testament times the temple priest—not the sinner— inspected the sacrifice. The goodness in Christ is greater than the badness in you."

The promises of forgiveness given to people of the Old Testament were a credit card on the payment Christ would make on the cross. The promises of forgiveness given to God's people after the Cross are Platinum debit cards, good anywhere.

When you praise and give thanks, you are praying. And prayer includes praise and thanksgiving. They are not separate entities. Even as the worst sinner begs forgiveness, he can immediately thank God for the forgiveness he's received. He can hold his head high, knowing that no matter how heinous his sin might have been, it has been dumped in the bottom of the deepest part of the sea.

One of my favorite anecdotes was about a saint who loved to praise God. No matter what the newly appointed preacher said each week, this dear, old saint would bellow, "Praise God!" Many of the members of the congregation found this habit irritating. Even the pastor would occasionally lose his train of thought upon hearing the man's sincere "Praise the Lord."

The minister tried talking to the man about it, but the man only looked bewildered. "But, Preacher, I can't help it. I am so full of gratitude for what God has done, I can't keep quiet."

One day the regional bishop was going to be in church to evaluate the young preacher's sermon. To avoid being derailed by the old man, the pastor caught up with him coming into church that morning. He explained about the visiting dignitary and then handed the man a *National Geographic* magazine and asked him to sit in the annex and read the magazine during the worship service.

The minister's sermon was going well. As he built toward the sermon's dramatic climax, he heard a loud and familiar, "Praise the Lord," come from the annex. And then a second, "Praise God. Thank You, Jesus."

After finishing his presentation, the pastor hurried to the annex. "What in the world did you find in that magazine to praise God over?"

"I couldn't help myself, Pastor. Look, it says right here that the Mariana Trench in the western Pacific Ocean is 36,000 feet deep. That's where God has thrown my sins! Doesn't that just make you want to praise God?"

It is easy to forget that, once forgiven, our sins are forever thrown into the depths of the sea (see Micah 7:19). When the devil comes calling, he's dressed for deep-sea diving. And if we let him, he will destroy the gratitude and the joy that come with forgiveness.

It is God's grace that allows us to live free. It's His grace that allows us to move beyond our past.

For many years, I had a reoccurring nightmare that brought back memories of my less than stellar youth, events that I had already carried to the throne of grace and deposited at the Savior's feet. I would awaken from this dream in tears. I would beg for God's forgiveness all over again; I would pray for joy; I would beg for the peace that comes from the Holy Spirit's presence in my life, but I couldn't shake the oppressive sadness I still felt hours later.

One morning following the dream's reoccurrence, the Holy Spirit led me to a text that would revolutionize my life. "I am focusing my energies on this one thing: Forgetting the past and looking forward to what lies ahead, I strain to reach the end of the race and receive the prize for which God, through Jesus Christ, is calling us up to heaven" (Philippians 3:13, 14, NLT).

Just as I can choose to praise God instead of complaining; just as I choose to love the Lord even when I don't feel like it; so I can choose to forget that which is in my past—it's forgiven and done! I can savor the moment of forgiveness; I can fall on my face with thanksgiving; and then I can press forward toward my glorious future with Jesus. Using the same key I use to break other destructive habits that try to strangle my growth, I can ask the Holy Spirit to alert me before I think the first self-destructive thought.

Come on, Kay, you protest, "You can't control dreams and nightmares." I know for a fact that you can. When I choose to go to bed praising God, I will awaken in the morning with praise on my lips. If worry is my demon of choice, I go to sleep reciting Psalm 23 or Psalm 91, and I will meet the dawn rejoicing.

The secret to using this key successfully is to continue to use it throughout the day. Each time a negative thought enters my mind, I thank God for His incredible forgiveness and grace, and then, I physically turn away from where I am standing or sitting and quote the first part of the verse, "I choose to forget that which is behind. I move on in God's oh so amazing grace." Try it. It works. At first you will find yourself needing to repeat the exercise several times a day, but after a while the frequency of negativity taking root in your mind will lessen; and joy and peace will return.

Now when memories of my worst mistakes return—and they still do—instead of weeping, I rejoice and praise my God for the awesome privilege of being His imperfect vessel in a broken world. "Give thanks in all circumstances, for this is God's will for you in Christ Jesus" (1 Thessalonians 5:18).

See how praise, gratitude, prayers of requests, and prayers of petition are so tightly interwoven that they cannot be separated? It's the Bible promises that add the tensile strength to the golden cords of worship. There are 8,000 of them! That's right—8,000 promises! (Someone actually counted them.) And they're all recyclable. Talk about a reason to rejoice!

GRACE NOTES

- Sing your favorite praise chorus or put a praise CD on your stereo and rejoice.
- Record in your praise journal or on tape humorous incidents from your childhood or from the lives of your children or grandchildren that give you fresh glimpses of God.
- Make a list of all your worst sins. Be honest with yourself. Ask the Holy Spirit to direct you. Place a check beside the sins for which you've asked and received forgiveness. Clear up any remaining sin with God. Now tear the list into tiny pieces; and last, throw the pieces into the bin for nonrecyclable trash and walk away—forever!
- Tell someone about God's incredible grace in your life.

PRACTICING GOD'S PRESENCE

You have made known to me the path of life;
you will fill me with joy in your presence,
with eternal pleasures at your right hand
(Psalm 16:11).

Have you ever heard a worshiper say, "God really showed up this morning, didn't He?" Does God show up in our worship services, or is it just a figure of speech? We talk about the presence of God, and we sing about it—"Surely the Presence of the Lord is in this Place." The morning invocation invites God into our worship service. But do we really want His presence?

Christian theology teaches that God is omnipresent—always present everywhere. Regardless of the feelings you and I might have at any particular moment, we are constantly in the presence of God. Feelings have never been the criterion for making an informed judgment. When our faith is weak, we often can't sense His presence. And that is not accurate since He is everywhere, all the time. Perhaps our prayer should be for God to make His presence known, to make us aware that He is truly with us.

The Bible gives many examples of people who found themselves in the presence of God. Adam and Eve heard the voice of God as He walked in the Garden at the end of the day. They fled from Him after they sinned. We are told that Enoch walked with God, as did Noah. Abraham was called a "God's friend" in James 2:23. Jacob wrestled with God. You can't get much closer than that. Moses and Joshua talked with the Lord. The psalmist wrote, "Where can I go from your Spirit? Where can I flee from your presence?" (Psalm 139:7). North, South, East, West—as far as one can travel, there God is.

Cosmonauts claimed to look for God in outer space, but didn't find Him. New Agers advise their followers to look inside themselves. "God is in you, and you are one and the same." However, while it's true that Jesus said the kingdom of God is in you, that God is with us and we are constantly in His presence, God and humans are still separate entities. We are not God.

"Come near to God and he will come near to you" (James 4:8). This invitation is always open. To launch this special relationship, all you have to do is start talking with Him. Tell Him about your day. He is there; He's interested; He's listening. Another way to enter into His presence is to meditate on a scripture text that turns your thoughts toward Him. "Taste and see that the LORD is good" (Psalm 34:8). Take time to savor the flavor.

Like the psalmist, I enjoy singing to the Lord. I think of my dad whenever I hear someone sing "No One Ever Cared for Me Like Jesus." My father loved that song. Another of his favorites was "How Great Thou Art." Though he couldn't carry a tune, I remember him saying that when he got to heaven, he would join a mass choir. There would be 1,000 sopranos, 1,000 altos, 1,000 tenors, and him. His voice would be so powerful that he could carry the bass part alone. Memories of my dad bring the image of my heavenly Father into focus faster than a thousand and one sermons.

Music brings me into my Beloved's presence faster than any other medium. There are praise choruses that force me to my knees. There are hymns that cause me to fall prostrate at His feet. One hundred and seventy times the term *sahah*, "to worship, prostrate oneself, bow down" is mentioned in the Hebrew Bible. Abraham "bowed" himself to the ground before the three messengers who announced that Sarah would have a son (see Genesis 18:2).

In the New Testament, the Greek word *proskuneo* means to reverence or to kiss. Revelation 4:10 describes the twenty-four elders falling down and worshiping the Lord. Revelation 7:11 shows the angels falling down on their faces before Him and worshiping Him. When was the last Sabbath morning you worshiped by bowing with your face to the floor before the altar?

Jesus used the Greek term *doxazo*, "to magnify, extol, to praise." " 'You are the light of the world. . . . Let your light so shine before men, that they may see your good deeds and praise your Father in heaven' " (Matthew 5:14, 16). Paul used it when he wrote Romans 15:6, "So that with one heart and mouth you may glorify the God and Father of our Lord Jesus Christ."

Isaiah 40:9 speaks of lifting one's voice in worship. "You who bring good tidings to Zion, go up on a high mountain. You who bring good tidings to Jerusalem, lift up your voice with a shout, lift it up, do not be afraid."

Reminding myself of God's nearness is an enjoyable worship exercise. Is there any reason God can't be sitting on the sofa or in my husband's rocker-recliner when I chat with Him at the end of my day? One of my favorite venues for meeting with God is while taking a stroll together. Walking side by side along the seashore or climbing over the rocks in the Sierra Nevada foothills makes the walk and the worship more intimate.

Another way I can enjoy the Master's presence is by imagining myself as a participant in the scripture narrative that I am reading. For instance, when a woman caught in adultery was thrown at His feet, I become that woman. I imagine how mortified I would have felt having all the good church people of the community gawking at me, judging me. Then I switch parts and imagine what the good women of the city were thinking as the drama played out before them. I listen to their gossiping tongues and contribute my own share of poison to the conversation. And what went through the minds of the men of the church who dragged the prostitute from her bed? Did they feel justified in their actions? How did the head elder look at her? Did he have a niggling guilt? Did he have second thoughts? If so, what were they? Did the "john," who allowed himself to be the Pharisees' stooge, stick around long enough to regret his actions? Did he ever seek out another prostitute? Then I apply what I've learned about myself to my present-day circumstances. Who am I judging too harshly? How would I feel if the worst of my most recent ten sins was broadcast in the church foyer on Sabbath morning?

Another example of enjoying the Master's presence is to read the closing scenes of the book of Revelation and picture it happening live and in living color. What will it be like to look up and see Jesus coming for you? Can you see Him placing a golden crown on your head? Can you see yourself casting that crown at His feet? When marching side by side through the gates into the city, who is on your right side? Who is on your left?

Revelation 3:21 says, " 'To him who overcomes, I will give the right to sit with me on my throne.' " See yourself seated next to the Father in His mighty throne. Feel the texture of the chair. What does it look like? Who is waiting at the foot of the throne for his turn? Look at the Father's face? Who does He look like? I once heard a preacher say that God's face will be the face of your worst enemy. What does that thought do to your psyche? The possibilities are endless. And each one brings us into His presence to glorify His holy name.

An Old Testament approach to worship can be found in recalling your family or national history, your past—the good times and the bad. Psalm 136 is an example.

Remembering the trials He has brought you through will evoke a fresh flood of gratitude and praise.

Whatever methods you use to enter into His presence, it is vital to remember that how you or I get there isn't as important as getting there and staying there as long as possible. What a privilege it is to dwell in the presence of God, to interactively worship with Him.

One word of caution: It is a wonderful thing when we have an emotional experience in the presence of God. But never forget that—even when we don't have an emotional experience, even when we don't "feel" His presence, He is still there.

Our highest calling is to glorify God. Worshiping Him is our purpose. Whatever else may be your calling in life, it is secondary to this. What an incredible circle of love: The more we behold Him, the more we love Him. The more we love Him, the more we want to worship Him; the more we worship Him, the more like Him we become. The more like Him we become, the more others see Him in us and the more we glorify His name. Like a Möbius band, there is no end.

It is awesome to imagine that we not only have the privilege, but we have a right to come into the presence of the mighty God. "Come boldly to the throne," He invites. He is the King of the universe, the Lord of lords! How can we come boldly? Talk about intimidation!

David was afraid to come before the Lord after being confronted by his sin. He prayed, "Cast me not away from thy presence; and take not thy holy spirit from me" (Psalm 51:11, KJV).

If you have ever felt overwhelmed by God's greatness, tell Him. If you've ever been terrified to stand before the One who knows every detail of your life, tell Him. Voice your fears. Ask Him to help you know Him beyond the grandeur of an Eternal God. Ask Him to help you see the Unseen. He wants you to view Him more clearly. It's the father of darkness, not the Father of light, who works to keep you from beholding the Creator's glory. He wants us to see Him with our hearts and not our eyes.

Because of disobedience, Adam and Eve were expelled from the Garden and denied face-to-face communion with God (see Genesis 3). Their son Cain also went out from the presence of the Lord (see Genesis 4). And we all remember the story of Jonah, who "[fled] ... from the presence of the LORD" (Jonah 1:3, NKJV).

Deliberate sin is the only way we can flee God's presence. Yet in the face of absolute rejection, heaven's hounds will continue to track God's runaways. Philippians 1:6 speaks to the hearts of the vilest of sinners and to the humblest of saints. "Being confident … that he who began a good work in you will carry it on to completion until the day of Christ Jesus."

After her husband died, Elaine struggled to raise their young daughter in the ways of God. But sixteen-year-old Cindy, restless to be free and to experience life, ran away with a friend to Hollywood, hoping to become an actress. Soon after, Elaine learned from one of Cindy's friends that Cindy was working in a strip bar in the worst part of Los Angeles and that she was on drugs. Elaine's first instinct was to rush down there and rescue her daughter. Cindy's friend advised against it.

"She told me to tell you that if you try to find her, she'll run away again. And next time she won't send someone to let you know where she is."

The grieving mother turned to her spiritual "Husband" for counsel. "Be still and know" was the advice she received. Nothing could have been more difficult for her to do, but Elaine chose to obey. Her prayers went from begging that God bring Cindy home, to rejoicing that her daughter was still alive, to vowing to wait patiently on the Lord.

One night, about a year after the girl left home, Elaine awoke in the middle of the night with an overwhelming sense that she should pray for Cindy. Kneeling beside Cindy's bed, she pled with God for her daughter. "I don't know what's happening Lord, in my daughter's life, but please be with her. Keep her safe."

At the same moment, Cindy was on stage, dancing in little more than a G-string, when a loud voice told her she was in danger; that she should get out of the bar and go home. "This is your last warning. If you don't listen, you will die."

The girl rushed off the stage in the middle of her number, threw on a T-shirt and a pair of sweat pants, hopped in her boss's Cadillac, and drove home. Throughout the three-hour drive home, the voice kept repeating the message, "You will die, Cindy. You will die!" The girl walked into the house and found her mother asleep on her knees beside Cindy's bed.

Later they learned that the girl's employer, whose advances she had spurned, had planned to kill her that night—until she took his car. The next morning a young police officer friend of Elaine's returned the automobile to the owner with the advice to leave the under-age Cindy alone or he'd personally see that the man was prosecuted to the fullest extent of the law. Today you wouldn't know Cindy. She finished high school, married the police officer, and together they are raising three young children in the Lord.

As Yogi Berra was rumored to have said about the game of baseball, "It ain't over 'til it's over." While the war of the worlds was won at Calvary, the battle for your child's soul "ain't over 'til it's over." I don't know which of God's resources will reach your child's heart, but I do know that the God who set the worlds into motion, the One who gave up everything so you and I could live—I am persuaded that He will use every tool imaginable to save your child until the day of Christ Jesus arrives. Parents of adult children can rejoice, for God will continue the good work He began in that boy or girl, man or woman. God loves him or her as much today as He did when that tiny one first lisped the name of Jesus. And the loving Father will continue reaching, drawing, and coaxing your precious one back to Him until the return of Christ Jesus. If that truth doesn't give you more than a passing pleasure of living in the essence of God's presence, I don't know what will.

We've discussed talking to God, moving into His presence, resting in His presence. What about hearing His response? There are several ways to "hear" God's voice. Journaling while dialoguing with God by using a question-and-answer format helps many worshipers better focus on their task. If journaling is for you, begin by asking God for His protection and His anointing. He will clear your mind.

"Lord, what is Your will about _____?" (Fill in the blank with whatever situation applies to your life.) Write down the thoughts that come into your mind. You may be surprised to learn how much He wants to tell you. Test your notes against Scripture; throw out anything that is not true to His Word. If nothing comes, He might be saying, "Be still, and know that I am God" (Psalm 46:10). This isn't a refusal to help you; it's simply advice to wait, to trust Him. This is the time to praise Him for His faithfulness. Focus your energies on His promises. Your faith will grow with every song of praise. And in His time, He will lead you into all truth.

A good example of God's perfect timing took place at Jerusalem's gate called Beautiful (see Acts 3). This was the favorite entrance to the temple court. It is believed to be the bronze-sheathed gate that led out of the court of the Gentiles to the court of the women (NIV Study Bible, p.1648).

For years, the lame man begged by the gate Beautiful before being healed. Jesus had walked through that gate many times and had not healed the man. Yet later, when Peter and John came along and the man asked for alms, Peter said, "I don't have a nickel to my name, but what I do have, I give you: In the name of Jesus Christ of Nazareth, walk!" (Acts 3:6, *The Message*). Peter gave him much more than the lame man imagined—the use of his legs. Can you imagine the dance he did in the temple of the Lord?

As a result of his healing occurring at this precise moment in time, thousands heard the name of Jesus and the message of salvation. God's perfect timing. Was the man's wait worth it? Only eternity will reveal how many lives were changed that day.

God uses our own thought patterns to speak to us when we tune into Him. He speaks to us through the peace He plants in our hearts. With practice we can learn to distinguish our own thoughts from His. Similar to the way Richard quieted Kelli with his love, God washes over our frantic spirits, and peace settles in our hearts. Because Satan is the author of confusion and discord, we can be certain that the shower of peace in our souls is from God.

Quieting the heart involves rejecting all violent emotions, such as anger, jealousy, bitterness, and any other works of the flesh (Galatians 5:19). They are high-ticketed luxuries a child of God cannot afford if he wants to clearly hear God's voice. To defeat these negative emotions, we must ask for healing. In Psalm 103, God promises to heal our diseases and forgive our sins. He is in the business of healing diseases and purifying hearts. "Let us draw near to God with a sincere heart in full assurance of faith, having our hearts sprinkled to cleanse us from a guilty conscience and having our bodies washed with pure water" (Hebrews 10:22).

Here's the text again in *The Message* paraphrase: "So friends, we can now—without hesitation—walk right up to God, into 'the Holy Place.' Jesus has cleared the way by the blood of his sacrifice, acting as our priest before God. The 'curtain' into God's presence is [Christ's] body" (Hebrews 10:19-22).

You and I can't completely understand how we can draw near to God and yet, at the same time He lives in our hearts. It sounds like a paradox, but it's not; it's interactive worship again. As we choose to dwell in the essence of His presence, God chooses to make His home in us.

He tells us we're temples of the Holy Spirit. How comfortable do we make it for Him? Does He have access to every room, every closet, and every cubbyhole? Do we make Him feel welcome? What about the decorations? Are they to His liking? The music? The conversations He overhears?

If He truly is the most important Guest in the universe, you and I will want Him to feel at home. We will ask Him to organize our appointment calendar so that we have more time to spend with Him. We'll put Him in charge of our video and DVD library, our CDs, and our collection of "treasured memories." We will not run around in a frenzy like Martha, worrying about what to serve or how to serve it, but we'll sit beside Mary at His feet.

Following a sermon on the story of Mary and Martha, a friend once commented, "If Martha had seated herself on the floor beside Mary, who would have fixed dinner for the crowd?" Good question. How many people was she serving? Thirteen, counting Jesus, plus three family members, plus the other women—the number could have exceeded thirty. Honestly, I'm not sure I could keep from becoming unglued at such a prospect.

When I thought about my friend's question, I wondered what other ways the Savior could have employed to ease Martha's work load. Perhaps the Creator of the universe would have whipped up a fabulous meal Himself—something quite heavenly—a culinary feast to remember. Perhaps He would have helped Martha prepare the meal. Can you hear Jesus talking about the kingdom as He slices the tomatoes for a tossed salad? Or seasoning the roast with heavenly garnishes?

The name Martha doesn't need to be on our birth certificate for us to limit God's creative power. I know more than a few of Martha's male counterparts who pull out their hair each month trying to pay the bills. Perhaps a few minutes sitting at His feet and listening to the Master's voice would reveal new and unexpected solutions to what seem like unconquerable situations.

Jesus comes to my heart and to yours for the same reason He came to Mary, Martha, and Lazarus's home—to spend time with those He loves. Well-meaning but misguided Martha missed the point of Christ's visits. While no serious Christian seeks to displease the Lord, we may, like Martha, be focusing on activity rather than relationship. If we frantically run about each week at church, doing first one good thing and then the next, we may miss the fact that God was present at the morning's services. Bible studies, good works, and evangelizing the world are all secondary to spending time at Jesus' feet, concentrating on His goodness and focusing on His love.

A wife can be so busy making a lovely home for her husband and children that she forgets her primary purpose. A husband can work so hard to bring in extra money to give his spouse beautiful things that he forgets to give her what she really needs—him. While I know this is an outdated stereotype of marriage—that the husband earns the money and the wife spends it, the point is still evident. Romance cannot survive on busyness or on the purchase of a new SUV. A good marriage thrives on intimacy. I once heard a Christian marriage counselor say,

"Intimacy isn't the marriage; it's merely the oil that keeps the machine running smoothly."

Intimacy with God keeps the rest of our lives running smoothly. First Corinthians 10:31 says, "So whether you eat or drink or whatever you do, do it all for the glory of God." Nothing is exempt from glorifying God. This is our destiny; our purpose for being.

Doing everything to the glory of God implies three things: First, I must take the time to find out what God wants for me each day. This is my quiet time with Him—the intimacy part of our relationship. Second, I must take the time to learn how He wants the job done. I need the wisdom of the Father to know how to carry out His will. Third, after I've prayed over what I believe God wants me to do and He's shown me how to go about it, then it's time to get busy and do it. Grandiose plans, if not acted on, will not get the job done.

Take for instance, writing books. I love to write books. I love to brainstorm book ideas with Richard. At any one time I have five or six full-blown book ideas floating around in my head. I probably won't live long enough to write every one of them. Before I finish one manuscript there are several more begging for my attention. But a book doesn't get written by planning only. Before I can get serious about a book idea, I must be certain that it is God's plan for me to write it. As a new writer, I thought I had to accept every writing assignment offered to me. I didn't dare pass on one. What if another opportunity never came along? Seventeen years into the business, I now know there will always be more book ideas and more stories to be told. Now I also know that there are sometimes other authors who might be better suited for a particular assignment than I am.

When deciding to write a particular book, I must first take the idea to God for His approval. Whenever I've run ahead of Him, I've regretted it later. Second, I wait for Him to tell me how to write the book. Should the manuscript be written in a chronological story format? Should it be written as a topical or a worship book? What information should be included in the story? What is the theme He wants me to emphasize? The best format for the material isn't always what I first imagined. I need God to guide me with each of these decisions.

And, third, I must, sooner or later, stop planning and settle down to my computer to write the book. Until I have sentences and paragraphs on my computer screen, all my time spent planning matters little more than a puff of hot air.

The same is true in my spiritual life. God must be my Inspiration and my Organizer. Yet as much as I enjoy the planning stage, I must take the next step. I must carry out His directives.

God wants us to be as prompt to listen to His voice as the boy Samuel: "Speak [Lord]; for thy servant heareth" (1 Samuel 3:10, KJV). He wants us to be ready, like the teenage Mary, to obey His call: " 'Let it be to me according to your word' " (Luke 1:38, NKJV). And I must have the disposition to follow His will as did Joseph when the angel told him to take Mary and the Child and flee to Egypt.

Interactive worship is beautiful, elevating, refreshing. But is that all there is? Does the aura of His presence have to stop with the final amen? That would be like throwing a wedding without a real marriage follow-up; or enjoying a two-week honeymoon without continuing with a lifetime of loving one another. The secular world offers nanoseconds of happiness, Kodak™ moments, or Disneyland days. Nothing lasts; satisfaction is temporary. In contrast, God's promises for a wellspring of love, an ocean of peace, a deluge of joy, and unending faith and hope last forever. It's so simple. " 'Remain in me' " (John 15:4).

Christ knew His time on earth was ending. Before He left, He wanted His disciples to understand that they could remain in His love. The night before His crucifixion, Jesus said, "If you remain in me and my words remain in you, ask whatever you wish, and it will be given you. . . . Now remain in my love" (John 15:7, 9).

Once you've found this incredible love, this unbelievable joy, stay put! That's what the word *remain* means, "abide or stay put." As a child I knew that when my mother said, "Stay put," she meant "Don't go anywhere! Don't move a muscle!"

Good advice. When you experience the essence of His presence in your life, stay put. Go to the store, but stay put in His presence. Pick up the dry cleaning, but abide in Him. Drop off the kids at soccer practice, but remain in His love.

One way you can abide in His love is by capitalizing on your weaknesses. We all have them, little bugaboos in our lives, pebbles in your sandals, gnats buzzing about your nose. Native tendencies, finely tuned bad habits can become the means by which you can continually remain in His love. Here's how it works. If you need patience, pray for humility. If you are prone to worry, pray for trust. If people irritate you, pray for kindness. If or when you sin, you can offer a prayer of confession and gratitude for God's forgiveness. And with each victory, you are ready to celebrate with your Father. This is how you can cultivate the spirit of constant prayer. As you do, you are interweaving your active life with your prayer life. Best of all the very temptations that once debilitated you become opportunities to strengthen your union with God. These victories are kisses of love to the Savior. Before you are aware of the changes, you will be praying constantly, not merely with words but with action. Nothing gives God more cause for celebration than when one of His children, by the grace of Jesus Christ, throws Satan's best efforts back in his face.

Living beautifully and loving it in the essence of His presence is not a dream or a fairy tale. It's a choice. Regardless of the bad times, and there will be bad times; regardless of our losses, and there will be losses; regardless of the hurt, the pain, or loneliness you and I may experience before He takes us home with Him, we can choose to remain in Him every moment of every day. This life-focusing experience is a breath away, as near as a prayer on our lips.

"You are so beautiful, Lord. Basking in the essence of Your presence is all I seek. Thank You for showing me how to live beautifully in You. You are my heart's desire. Purify my heart. Arrange my life the way You want it to be. You know my weaknesses and You understand my failings. Should I wander off, please draw me back once again to the reality of Your love.

"Today I choose to sit at Your feet; today I choose to look deep into Your love-filled eyes and inhale Your exquisite aroma. Today I choose to listen while You speak to me. Hold me Lord, today."

GRACE NOTES

- Set your alarm a half hour earlier than usual. Before leaving your bed, luxuriate in the new day by stretching your limbs slowly. Sing or recite your favorite psalm as you begin to stir. Be still and experience God's presence.
- Mark the seasons with childhood praise. If it's springtime, go fly a kite; summer, build a sand castle; in the fall, rake a pile of leaves and jump into them; and should it be winter, take a walk in a snowstorm and let the flakes melt on your tongue, all the while praising your Creator Father.
- Make a "today" prayer list of the names of those individuals who irk you. Lift up each of these people to God for an extra-special blessing.
- List the luxuries in your life which you can no longer afford if you want to experience the essence of God's presence.
- Read Psalm 136. Beginning with the tenth verse, paraphrase your own list of victories you've experienced in Jesus.

END NOTES

Quest for Contentment
1. Noble Alexander and Kay D. Rizzo, *I Will Die Free* (Nampa, Idaho: Pacific Press Publishing Association, 1992), 73, 74.

Dying of Thirst
1. W. E.Vine, Merrill F. Unger, William White, jr. eds. *Vine's Expository Dictionary of Biblical Words* (Nashville, Tenn.: Thomas Nelson Publishers), 284, 285.

2. Vine.

3. Carolyn and Joseph Grassi, *Mary Magdalene and the Women in Jesus' Life* (Lanham, Md.: Sheed and Ward, 1986), 65.

4. Ellen G. White, *The Ministry of Healing* (Nampa, Idaho: Pacific Press Publishing Association, 1942), 237.

5. Alexandra Stoddard, *Living a Beautiful Life* (New York: Avon Books, 1986), 126.

Playing Hide-and-Seek
1. Edward B. Burger and Michael Starbird, *The Heart of Mathematics: An Invitation to Effective Thinking* (Emery, Calif.: Key College Publishing, 2000), 47-50.

2. Burger.

Who's Seeking Whom?
1. J. I. Packer, Merrill C. Tenney, William White, Jr., *The Bible Almanac* (Nashville, Tenn.: Thomas Nelson Publishers, 1980), 491.

God and Infinity

1. "Song of Solomon: A Song of Love," *Adult Sabbath School Bible Study Guide* by Ronald Flowers and associates. Pacific Press Publishing Association. October-December 1992, 22.

2. Flowers.

3. *The Interpreter's Bible,* 5:102.

4. Ellen G. White, *Steps to Christ* (Silver Spring, Md.: Review and Herald Publishing Association, 1892), 10.

Secure in the Essence of His Presence

1. Oswald Chambers, *My Utmost for His Highest* (Grand Rapids, Mich.: Discovery House Publishers, 1935), 332.

To the Heart of Worship

1. Vine, 196, 197.

Recipes for Worship

1. Kathleen Norris, *Amazing Grace: A Vocabulary of Faith* (New York: The Berkley Publishing Group, 1998), 207.

2. Gary Thomas, *Sacred Pathways: Discover Your Soul's Path to God* (Nashville, Tenn.: Thomas Nelson Publishers, 1996).

3. Thomas, 30.

4. Thomas, 23, 24.

5. Thomas, 34, 35.

6. Thomas, 259, 260.

More Than a Chorus Line

1. Peter Bath, "Show Us Your Glory: Corporate Worship and the Complete Christian," *Adventist Review* (May 2002), 35-37.

2. Norris, 246.

3. Norris, 151.

STUDY GUIDE

Each of these short studies is designed to help you digest and apply the ideas developed in this book and to direct you back to Scripture, the ultimate source of truth.

Living the More Abundant Life

1. In "Living the More Abundant Life," the author explores human reality. What is your reality? How does your temporary grasp on reality compare with God's eternal reality of living an abundant life? How does having read the last chapter of God's book help you deal with the temporary realities of living in a chaotic world?

   A. What Scripture texts would you use to compare human-kind's temporary condition with God's eternal? Begin with 1 Corinthians 13:12, KJV.

   B. If Eve had a Garden of Eden Prayer Journal, what might she include in it? How would her daily entries differ from yours?

   C. How do you view earlier eras? How would you apply Christ's promise of a more abundant life (John 10:10) to a person walking the Oregon Trail in the early 1800s? To a person facing the Inquisition? To a U.S. soldier in Vietnam?

   D. List examples of times when the Creator lavished unrestrained abundance on His people.

   E. Read Isaiah 64:4 and 1 Corinthians 2:9. Try to wrap your mind around the vastness of these words. Regardless of how far your mind takes you, the Father's reality goes further. What outrageous acts of compassion has the Creator of the universe bestowed on you?

2. During a time of despair in the author's life, she admitted that the idea of living an abundant life was beyond her wildest imagination. "It wasn't until much later that I discovered I needed to become disillusioned with everything I had once believed before I was ready to listen to God." How do you feel about this statement? Does it apply to every Christian? Explain. Recall a time when God used your anger or your pain to begin your healing.

A. Read Psalm 58:5-7 and Psalm 57:7-11 for an example of a cursing psalm and a praise psalm. How does praising God change one's grief to joy?

B. "My heavenly Father didn't change His message; He changed me." What hope can the habitual whiner, the chronic complainer, and the dissatisfied critic find in this statement?

C. "Attitude is everything!" Do you believe this statement to be true? What does Paul say about maintaining a positive attitude?

D. Jesus said, "I tell you the truth, you will weep and mourn while the word rejoices. You will grieve, but your grief will turn to joy" (John 16:20). At what point does one's grief turn to joy? When Jesus returns for His faithful? When we turn our grief over to our Father? Give a scriptural example to support your position. (Recall the fruit of the Spirit.)

E. Consider the story of the Irishman eating alone in his room. Do you sometimes feel as if everyone is dining at God's table except you? Are you settling for a stale-bread relationship with God instead of feasting on His bounty? If so, why?

F. Is it possible for genuine heirs of God's kingdom to completely miss out on the abundance He has for them in this life and still inherit the next? Is it possible for God's child to think of himself as one of this world's homeless poor and, at the same time, know he is one of God's wealthiest heirs?

G. When the disciples returned to the well and asked Jesus if He was hungry, He replied, "I have food of which you know nothing." Of what food was He speaking? What text assures us that we too can enjoy such food?

Quest for Contentment, Search for Satisfaction

1. "We will be content" (1 Timothy 6:8). Compare the words *contentment* and *satisfaction* with what is happening in your life. How content are you in your present condition? How willing are you to remain in your present situation until God finishes the work He is doing in and for you? Where does contentment stop and complacency begin?

   A. Considering the condition of the world today, what is your reaction to Psalm 37:24-26? How would a Christian in Rwanda or Liberia read this promise? Are Christians always spared death by starvation? If not, why not? Where does trust end and presumption begin?

   B. Many unbelievable stories have come out of the 9/11 tragedy. Concrete and steel beams fell on good folk as well as bad. One Christian man left home that morning wearing a new pair of shoes. He hadn't gone far when a blister formed on his heel. Stopping in a convenience store to purchase a Band-Aid, he missed his morning train. That five-minute delay saved his life. Was God watching over him but not over the fireman who kept returning into the building to save others and thereby lost his own life? Nonbelievers want to know. How do you answer the question of "Why do bad things happen to good people?" What promises from the Word would you use to support your position?

   C. While standing in a lake of sewer water, Humberto Noble Alexander asked, "Where is God in all of this?" God answered the faithful prisoner's question in a very graphic manner. Tell of a time in your life when God assured you that He was right beside you.

2. The author wrote about God's laws of gardening. "You will reap what you sow." What other laws of nature can apply to one's actions, whether one believes in God or not? Share an anecdote from

your experience that illustrates how God comes through for us when we are faithful to Him.

3. Reread Habakkuk 3:17, 18. What biblical principle does this passage illustrate?
   A. How does the prophet's attitude differ from the average person's today? What other biblical writers wrote about rejoicing despite their losses?
   B. There are times when God allows us to endure pain for the sake of growth. True or false? Give a personal example to support your position.

4. How far does a million dollars go in the twenty-first century? Would you eat a centipede for a million bucks? A school teacher and a millionaire businessman were discussing how much money would they each want to salt away before they could retire early. The school teacher's amount was mere pocket change to the businessman's. They came from totally different paradigms. What is your paradigm of contentment? How much more money a month would it take to make you financially content? What is your price?
   A. " 'Where your treasure is, there your heart will be also.' " Examine your motives for seeking a closer communion with God. What do you expect to get out of this relationship?
   B. Take this word-association quiz. To the following words and phrases, write down your first response: Jesus Christ, Holy Spirit, Father God, Second Coming, heaven, eternity, the new earth. What, if anything, did you learn about yourself?
   C. A popular movement in churches today claims that a person has the right to expect financial blessings. Do you agree that God's abundance always includes financial wealth? Support your belief with an example from the Word.

5. Name the fruit of the Spirit found in Galatians 5:22. The singular form of the word *fruit* is used, not the plural. Does that mean the Spirit's fruit comes as one package? Or does the Spirit of God give

the fruit to you one at a time? Love—peace—hope—patience—temperance, etc.

    A. Given a billion dollars, which of the fruit would you be willing to live without for all eternity?

    B. Compare the fruit of the Spirit and the Beatitudes of Matthew 5. How are they similar? If *blessed* means "happy," what can you derive from these comparisons?

Dying of Thirst

1. How does knowing that a descendant of Korah wrote Psalm 42 add more meaning to the psalm? Give an example of a time in your life when you were spiritually dry and dying of thirst. What other faithful men and women of the Bible experienced such a thirst for God?

    A. "Psalm 42's three-part structure—call to worship, confession of sin, and encouragement to trust God—is God's antidepressant for today's woes." Tell why you agree or disagree with this claim. How does worship lift the spirits of the depressed? Why must the confession of sin be included in the cure? And why must the ailing believer move from "worship to confession to trust" in order to experience a healing?

    B. How does the author's illustration of cleansing her grandsons' cuts and bruises with clean water relate to Psalm 42? Why must a wound be cleansed before it can heal properly?

2. What benefits can you see to a local church congregation in having both the fast-flowing water of committed youth and the silent waters of maturity? What drawbacks can you see to each position?

    A. "Age has little to do with spirituality." True or false? Give examples from the Word to illustrate your position. What can you learn from the author's ninety-year-old friend Minnie? What is God's true "Fountain of Youth"?

    B. Author Max Lucado writes, "It isn't the circumstance that matters; it's God in the circumstance." How does looking away from my temporal problem to the Problem Solver put my situation into proper perspective? How does this apply to cancer?

Death of a loved one? Isolation from family and friends? Give examples of people in the Bible whose experiences illustrate this principle.

3. Jesus waited at the well of Sychar for one particular woman. His life was controlled by His Father's will. He didn't just happen by the well that day. Christ was there by design. Can the same be true of your life and mine? Is each action, each encounter, and each detour we take a part of God's plan and not a stroke of good or bad luck? Do you agree or disagree?

   A. Is there, for Christians, the possibility of being in the wrong place at the wrong time? What texts would support your position?

   B. Read John 6:37-40, 44, 45. According to these verses, how do people come to Christ? What promise does Jesus make in verses 39 and 40? Is this a promise you can claim? Explain.

Playing Hide-and-Seek

1. What is your response to the concept that man is a spiritual being on a human journey and not a human on a spiritual journey? Does it agree or disagree with Scripture?

   A. In the Garden of Eden, the Creator took time out to walk with His newest creations. How can parents learn from the Father's behavior with Adam and Eve?

   B. Many Christians believe that God is playing hide-and-seek with His children. Do you picture the God of the universe playing games?

2. The author refers to Psalm 8:3, 4, as God's "chalk-marks" put there to guide us toward Him. In what natural wonders can you spot God's "chalk-marks"?

   A. What is your response to the idea that God used the same number pattern to grow hairs on your head as He used to mold a head of cabbage? Does it increase or decrease your faith in Him? What lesson can you take from Fibonacci's discovery? Does this discovery affect the ultimate value of a human being?

B. "God loves me so much that He would rather die than live forever in a perfect universe without me." How does the truth of this statement make you feel about yourself? How does it make you feel about your worst enemy?

C. Imagine knowing before you conceived your child that that little person would grow up to kill another human being. Would you think twice before beginning that child's life? Relate the analogy to God's creation of Lucifer.

D. Describe your feelings regarding the word *perish* in John 3:16 as meaning "self-destruct." Someone once said that all sin leads to death. What is your opinion regarding these two concepts?

E. What did you learn in this chapter about God's love?

F. Martha Williamson, of the television hit *Touched By an Angel,* once said, "God loves you; now deal with it." How do you "deal" with His love in your everyday life? With your spouse? With your children? With your parents? With your boss?

Who's Seeking Whom?

1. The Almighty is beyond our reach and exalted in power (Job 37:23). How does this text make you feel? If God is beyond our reach, why does humankind constantly search for Him?

   A. How would you feel if God were only toying with us, the way a cat might toy with a mouse or bird? How do you know that this is not the case?

   B. How do you balance the awesome power of the Lord of Creation with the compassion of Jesus?

2. In the four parables discussed in this chapter—the lost coin, the lost sheep, the prodigal son, and the pearl of great price—where can you best see yourself? When you picture God's role in each of the stories, what new insights about Him do you experience?

   A. "Obedience without love is slavery." Do you agree or disagree? How does the freedom God gives His kids exemplify His unconditional love? Why can't our bad choices diminish God's love for us? Why can't our goodness increase it?

B. How is the robe of Christ's righteousness a protection against the "law of the land"?

C. How does identifying yourself with the pearl of great price affect your view of God? Of yourself? Of others?

D. Do you ever feel like a commodity with everyone wanting a "piece of you"? What emotion do you experience when you consider your worth from a heavenly perspective?

3. "God's love could not save you." Explain your reaction to the statement. Do you agree or disagree?

4. Read Romans 8:38, 39. What does believing that you are never out of the Father's reach do to your confidence? Why is it sometimes difficult to embrace the fact that nothing can separate you from God's love?

God and Infinity

1. Read Psalm 36:7-9 in various translations and paraphrases. Discuss your response to the text.

2. "How exquisite your love, O God!" What does the word *exquisite* mean to you? How is God's love exquisite?

A. "How eager we are to run under your wings." How and when are you most eager to "run under His wings"?

B. "To eat our fill at the banquet you spread." Relate your best dining experience with the spiritual feast God places before you.

C. "As you fill our tankards with Eden spring water." Was the water Jesus used in the miracle at the wedding of Cana Eden's spring water? Bottling companies will go to great expense to advertise their product as being pure spring water. What value do you put on God's purest water?

D. "You're a fountain of cascading light, and you open our eyes to light." Could this picture be the rainbow described as being around His throne? How can God open your eyes to such a vision of beauty?

3. Read Psalm 139:1-6. Think back over your day's activities and your day's thoughts. How do you feel about God's reading your every thought today? Do you find it reassuring or disconcerting? Explain.

   A. Sooner or later we will each become an orphan from the human perspective. What promises can you quote that assures you that you can never really be an orphan?

   B. Have you ever fantasized about "flying on the wings of the morning"? Share your thoughts about someday flying with angels.

   C. "The days of my life all prepared [for me] before I'd even lived one day." How does this text relate to predestination? What scriptures would you use to explain this concept to a nonbeliever?

4. Try to wrap your mind around the concept of infinity for a moment. No beginning, no ending. Divide infinity in half and what do you have? Agape—God-love—is love-infinity. The Father didn't love you less yesterday than today, and He won't love you more or less tomorrow.

5. Is the reverse true? Can you love God more today than yesterday and less than you will tomorrow? Can your love for God ever completely be agape love? Why or why not?

6. We speak of "unconditional" love. Reread what Paul wrote about love in 1 Corinthians 13. Paraphrase it to fit your world.

7. "Loving someone in order to get something in return is prostitution." Strong words, shocking words. How do you feel about this analogy? How can it apply to the individual who uses God and heaven as a fire-insurance policy? Why is this self-serving position doomed to failure?

8. The author said she enjoys singing secular love songs to God. How do you feel about that? Can the lyrics of a love song between a man and a woman be appropriately transferred to a human wife and her heavenly Husband?

9. The Song of Solomon is an exquisite love story. It is also a pastoral poem and a dialogue between two lovers. Intellectually you may accept that it is also an allegory for your love-relationship with our Creator-Husband, but emotionally, how does it make you feel? How comfortable would you be to read it out loud during a church service? Explain.

   A. It can be said that knowledge without emotion is as dangerous as emotion without knowledge. Why? What are the dangers of elevating one's intellect above the emotions? What are the dangers of elevating emotions above one's intellect? What does God's Word say about each of these dangers?

   B. In intellect vs. knowledge, where and how does the Holy Spirit enter the equation? If God the Father speaks to man's mind; the Son lived in a man's physical body; and the Spirit communicates with His heart, what happens when we attempt to isolate or subject one of these facets of our person?

   C. True love cannot be intellectually quantified. There is no mathematical formula. Love is a God-thing. At some point the wisest, the most intelligent of individuals must take a leap of faith and love someone. What are the risks inherent in loving another human being? What are the risks of loving God completely?

   D. The three views of God revealed in the Song of Solomon are God as King and Ruler; as Friend and Brother; and as a passionate Lover. Why are some Christians reluctant to talk about God as our Lover? They are much more comfortable with the less intimate term *Beloved*. Do you believe that the analogy of God being our Lover is easier for women to accept than it is for men? If so, why? If not, why not?

   E. What holds you back from coming to your Bridegroom in complete surrender? Is it an issue of intimacy? Of loss of personal control?

   F. Imagine God seated on His throne, leaning forward, eagerly waiting to hear you say, "I love You!" Not as a rite of passage or a ritual part of your worship, but shouted with pure, unabashed joy. Share a time when you wanted the world to know how much you loved your Lord.

10. Intimacy with God is the purest form of worship. Mary bathed her Master's feet with perfume. She held nothing back. What kinds of things hold God's people back from completely abandoning themselves to worship?

Secure in the Essence of His Presence

1. What tragedy during your lifetime changed you forever? In what way? How did you put it into perspective with your relationship with God? Did you lose your way for a time? If so, how did you find Him again?

2. "Pursuing God can be forgotten in the glare of life's 'virtual reality.'" What is the difference between a virtual-reality experience, God's eternal view, and what is happening in your life today? What does it mean to "live above one's problems"?

   A. The apostle Paul learned to live above his situation (see Philippians 4:12, 13). What was his recipe for living?

   B. If you are living in the essence of God's presence, how do life's difficulties touch your life?

   C. "Wannabe Christians wear their religion like cheap cologne." Do you agree or disagree? Tell of a time when you were accosted by a brother's or a sister's personal brand of spiritual perfume (i.e. witness). How did you deal with the situation?

   D. "God's essence always draws and never repels." What can we learn from this statement? What text confirms your beliefs?

3. Consider Sandi's story. Does the voice on the phone line singing "Jesus Loves Me" seem too far-fetched to be believed? I like to think of this as a God-hug; as a moment God took away from the administration of the universe to reassure one of His frightened children. Tell of a time God gave you such a hug. What stories in the Bible would apply?

   A. Falling in love with God produced incredible changes in Sandi. Is Sandi's experience common to each of God's children? Can a person be in love and successfully hide it? Explain.

   B. The secret to living in the essence of His presence was illustrated by grandson Jarod's command to "Focus." Why is it necessary to focus all our attention on God before we can live in the essence of His presence?

4. "True worship is all about God, not about us." How does this statement affect your view of worship? Does it change your definition of worship? Does every church service automatically fit into the category of true worship?
   A. What does it mean to worship God "in spirit and in truth"? How does one do it?
   B. Do you ever find your mind wandering during your prayer time? How do you rein in an undisciplined mind? What advice would you give someone facing this problem?
   C. How will one's worship be enhanced by totally focusing on God?
   D. How should Jesus' need for a personal worship time with His Father influence your decision to come apart and worship Him?

To the Heart of Worship

1. In chapter 8 the author shared her conversion experience, the moment when she officially gave her heart to God. Tell about your own conversion experience. How vivid is the event in your memory? Share the sensory details as you remember them.
   A. Jesus told Nicodemus that he needed to be born again. Is it possible to love God without ever being "born again"? Why or why not?
   B. Can living in such a moment sustain a relationship? Explain.
   C. How does the "born again" experience affect one's future spiritual life?
   D. Think through your list of "to do's" for today. How can your every action be a praise to God? Is such a concept reasonable? Why or why not? What scripture would you use to support your belief?
   E. The author equates living in the essence of God's presence with her constant awareness of her love for her husband of forty years. Is the metaphor reasonable?
   F. Give examples of how God tucks love notes into your daily life.

2. True worship is not a spectator sport. Can you merely watch others
   worshiping God and receive a personal blessing? Explain.
   A. How do you define "interactive worship"? Is such an experi-
      ence scriptural?
   B. How does the concept of an interactive worship fit with the
      sensual nature of the Song of Solomon? Is there a place for
      such emotions in one's worship time?
   C. What is the difference between praying and worshiping?

3. Theologians have said that Zephaniah 3:14-17, is the Old Testa-
   ment equivalent of John 3:16. Do you agree or disagree? Why?
   A. How do you respond to the female orientation of this text?
      How does it affect your acceptance of it?
   B. Can you visualize God sitting on His throne? Does it make you
      uncomfortable to do so? Why? Is it dangerous to imagine that
      which we have not seen? Why or why not? Is it wrong to appre-
      ciate God's creative power working in our minds?

4. Of the Three Persons of the Godhead, the Holy Spirit is the One
   least understood. Do you agree or disagree? He is also the One who
   is physically closest to us, yet we sometimes fear Him. Why do you
   think that is so?
   A. How does the Holy Spirit participate in your personal worship
      time?
   B. What does it mean to be "led by the Spirit"?
   C. Have you ever experienced the Holy Spirit's presence in your wor-
      ship? What are the indications that assure you of His presence?

5. "Receiving the kingdom of God like a child." It has been said that
   the adult American society does not treasure children. They coddle
   them, spoil them, condescend to them, but they really do not like
   them. Do you agree or disagree? Why?
   A. Does the idea of becoming a child again seem frightening to
      you? Why?
   B. What is it about a child that Jesus commends? How does Paul's
      advice on spiritual maturity coincide?

C. When was the last time you enthusiastically rejoiced in God? What would happen if you abandoned your "proper demeanor" to do so?

6. Share a personal worshipful experience that has seen you through a difficult time? What song or scripture text do you associate with that experience?

7. What additional meaning does the phrase "He is mighty to save" have when you understand that *eager* is a synonym for *mighty*? When you think about whatever trouble you are facing, how does the picture of a God eager to rush to your aid affect your love for Him?

A. The author tells of imagining a giant chalkboard on which her mistakes are written down and must be cleared. Another belief she once held is the donkey-and-the-carrot analogy. Why is this view theologically right or wrong? What other misconceptions of God have you learned or rejected over the years? Why?

B. Recalling the story of the man digging up the gold on heaven's streets, what other values do people hold that will be upside-down and inside-out to what God values?

8. "He will take great delight in you." The word *great* implies a heightened intensity and the word *delight* means unbridled joy. How does such a picture of "great delight" affect your view of God?

A. It's easy to imagine yourself taking great delight in God and His awesome power, but how simple is it to realize that the opposite is also true? Can you picture God, as your Father, taking "intense, unbridled joy" in you?

B. Is imagining such a view of the eternal God too "relaxed" or somehow sacrilegious? Is there a danger inherent in "humanizing" God too much? Support your opinion with scripture.

C. Have you ever wondered if God had abandoned you? What promise could you give to a friend who felt as if his or her prayers weren't going beyond the ceiling?

D. How is your view of your heavenly Father affected by your view of your earthly father? Do you see God as an absent or distant parent? A demanding parent? A playful parent? An understanding parent? Share your insights.

9. " 'He will rejoice over you with singing.' " The Hebrew word for *rejoice (samah)* is so intense it must find expression in an external act. What images does God singing over you produce in your mind?

    A. Imagine God cheering for you. Why is it that Christians can cheer for their favorite baseball or football team and not for their Creator during a joyful song service?

    B. Why do Christians often picture the Father of all nations stoically watching over His kids from afar? Why do we have no problem picturing Him frowning or furious or disappointed, but seldom imagining Him laughing and enjoying the antics of His kids?

10. *I will bring you home.* Any parent who has had to leave a premature baby or a sick child in the hospital knows how eager God must be to take us home where we belong.

    A. What emotions would you use to ascribe to the Father on the Sunday morning before His Son returned home?

    B. How would you describe the Father on the morning before He comes back to take you home? Will His joy be explosive?

11. Tell how viewing worship from God's perspective enhances your own enjoyment of your special time with Him.

Recipes for Worship

1. How did the author's attitude regarding canned lentil soup strike you? Have you ever known anyone who took such a rigid position on the way things must be done? Explain.

    A. From broccoli to artichoke hearts, from beefsteak tomatoes to succulent Concord grapes, the varieties of good nutritious food given us by God seems endless. Jesus equated eating earthly food with ingesting heavenly sustenance. If we receive our spiritual nourishment through worship, how open should we be to experiencing a wide variety of heavenly food?

B. Expecting others to live exactly as you live, eat the same food, worship in the same way, is bondage. True or false? Explain.

C. "Too often worshiping in spirit and truth is diametrically opposed to our own culturally limited thinking." True or false. How much of your style of worship is inherited? Cultural? Habitual? Explain.

D. What boundaries did God put on humans' acts of worship?

2. Why is worshiping with other believers necessary to healthy spiritual growth?

A. What are the differences between personal and corporate worship?

B. What are the benefits received by worshiping in a body of believers?

C. Can these benefits be negated? How?

D. If the worship pattern in your church family doesn't agree with you, what can you do about it?

E. If an individual told you that he or she left church unfed and hungry each week and was considering attending a church of another faith, what would you advise that person to do?

F. Must corporate worship meet all your spiritual needs? If so, explain. If not, why?

3. In Amos 5:21, God says, "I hate, I despise your religious feasts; I cannot stand your assemblies." What was it about the worship of Amos's day that God hated?

A. Read 2 Timothy 3:5. Have you ever felt as if you were merely going through the motions of worshiping God? If so how did you deal with your problem?

B. How do you balance society's view of "proper religious decorum" with your concept of genuine worship?

C. Upon hearing a heartfelt song or a testimony, have you ever choked back your tears rather than let others know you were moved by the Spirit?

4. "Abraham ... built altars everywhere he went." Sounds like a man who cherished tradition. Do you find beauty, comfort, and order in the weekly traditions in your church?

    A. Our traditional hour of service was established by an agricultural society. It gave farmers time to finish their morning chores before attending church. Most of us no longer live on farms and have a heavy load of morning chores, yet we continue to worship at the same traditional times. What would be your reaction should the church board decide to change the 11:00 A.M. service to the 4:00 P.M. service to accommodate the parents of young children? Why? Would it be wrong?

    B. What are the benefits of maintaining a consistent structure in corporate worship? What are the drawbacks? Are the benefits and drawbacks the same in one's personal worship?

    C. How much change is too much? How does the sincere, unselfish traditionalist respond to other people's desire for change?

5. "Elijah's and Moses' conversations with God revealed streaks of activism." What does it mean to be an activist? Can an activist worship God through his causes? Did the encounter with King Agrippa engender a worship experience for the apostle Paul?

    A. "An Activist serves a God of justice." What other Bible crusaders found spiritual satisfaction in confrontation?

    B. "Pick your battles" is wise advice for all of God's children. Are we supposed to be spiritually confrontational with everyone we meet? When is debate appropriate?

    C. "Salvation is for lovers, not fighters." Do you agree or disagree? Explain.

    D. Sir Thomas More neither confronted nor crusaded against Henry VIII's right to divorce Catherine of Aragon to marry Anne Boleyn. He remained totally silent on the issue. His refusal to voice his position on the issue rang through the kingdom like church bells on Easter morning. Unable to break More's stubborn silence, the king executed him anyway. When is silence appropriate?

  E. How does an activist respond to a world of "political correct-
ness"?

  F. Do you ever feel guilty for not being more of an activist? Do
you shy away from spiritual activists? Why?

  G. What are the benefits and the dangers inherent in an activist's
choice of worship?

6. "The Naturalist receives the greatest blessing worshiping God in nature."

  A. Tell of a time or a place when your spirits soared in worship of
your Creator.

  B. What are the benefits of worshiping God in a natural setting?

  C. What are the limitations?

7. "The Sensate worshiper loves God through her senses." How well
do you relate to the sensate?

  A. Medical science tells us that the sense of smell is the strongest
of our five senses. How did Old Testament Israel include the
sense of smell in their worship?

  B. How was incense a part of the Old Testament sanctuary service?

  C. Is there a place for incense in today's worship? Why or why
not?

  D. List the limitations and the benefits of the sensate's worship
style.

8. "The Ascetic wants nothing more than to be left alone in prayer."
Music, other people, and outside trappings distract him from his
goal to worship God.

  A. Can you relate to this worship need? Have you ever experienced a "wilderness experience"? What did you learn?

  B. Try to put yourself back in first-century Israel. How would you
have received John the Baptist's unusual lifestyle?

  C. What are the benefits and the dangers for the ascetic worshiper?

9. "The Caregiver loves God best by loving others." Of all the worshipers described, this is the one the author admires the most. Mother Teresa's care-giving nature took her from Eastern Europe to Calcutta's dirty streets. She dared to touch the untouchables, to minister to those whom society classified as waste products.

    A. What feelings do you have regarding the caregivers of the world?
    B. The biblical example of a caregiver is Dorcas. She didn't meet the needs of the poor because she could sew. She used her talent for sewing to meet the needs of the poor. Lydia, the seller of purple, could meet the needs of the poor with her organizational skills or her wealth. How much does talent have to play with being a caregiver? In the popular vernacular, which came first, the chicken or the egg?
    C. When you see a homeless person on the street or when you see a child being mistreated, what is your initial response? What is likely to be your ultimate response?
    D. What are the dangers and the benefits to the caregiver's worship?

10. "The Contemplative loves God through contemplation." Worshiping Jesus at His feet, Mary illustrated the sincere contemplative worshiper.

    A. Biblical scholars claim the reason Mary was chosen to be the first to proclaim Jesus' resurrection was because she was the truest of Jesus' disciples. Do you agree or disagree? Explain.
    B. To the activist, the contemplative's worship experience might be interpreted as overly sentimental. How would you dispute or defend this viewpoint?
    C. What are the benefits and the dangers in contemplative worship?

11. "The Enthusiast loves God through mystery and celebration. . . . This is God's cheerleader." How do you relate to the enthusiastic worshiper? Would David's enthusiasm be acceptable in your weekly worship service? Why or why not?

   A. An enthusiast sees life as a series of miracles and God as a very personal Being. Her childlike trust is often misinterpreted by other worshipers as being naive. How do you view this style of worship?

   B. Is there a limit to the amount of celebratory worship you are willing to endure from the enthusiast?

   C. What dangers do you see inherent in the enthusiast's mode of worship?

   D. What are the benefits?

12. "The Intellectual loves God with his mind. Primarily he lives in a world of concepts." Does this describe you? Do you know a worshiper who qualifies for this category of worship?

   A. The book of Romans was written by the intellectual worshiper, the apostle Paul. Paul himself realized that at the Acropolis he tried to out-reason the intelligentsia of Greece. Later he vowed to speak only of Jesus and Him crucified. Why do you think he came to this decision?

   B. What are the dangers for the intellectual?

   C. What are the advantages?

13. It is said that Jesus' example embodied each of the nine worship patterns to express His love to His Father. Review the worship patterns again and choose events in Christ's life that illustrate each.

How does learning about the different pathways to worship that God's people have used throughout history enrich your worship choices?

   A. How many of the nine worship patterns best describe you? What are they?

   B. How does it help you to be more tolerant of those who worship God in a much different way than you do?

   C. What bridges can you make with those who differ from you?

   D. What new worship pathways are you open to trying?

The Elements of Effective Worship

1. What is the purpose of praise? How will beginning your planned worships with praise enhance your time spent with God?

    A. Read Psalm 145:1-7. Is praising for your benefit or for God's? Explain. Does God need our praises?

    B. Compare Psalm 145:10 with 1 Peter 2:9. How is praise a spiritual ID to the rest of the universe?

    C. "Praise is a choice a child of God makes every moment of every day." Why is it important to distinguish between gratitude and praise?

    D. How would determining to praise your family members and your co-workers change the atmosphere surrounding you?

    E. A person experiencing job burnout can greatly accelerate his healing by learning to praise. Why would this be true?

    F. Replacing complaining with praising is a habit worthy of cultivating. What other attitudes when replaced with praise would make you a gentler, more cheerful person?

2. "Despite all this adulation [by nature], it's your praise and mine that He most desires." What makes your praise (and mine) so unique and special to God?

    A. How can one's worship take on a "form of godliness" (see 2 Timothy 3:5)? Have you ever felt you were just "going through the motions," that your worship lacked power?

    B. Which of Scripture's 8,000 promises do you cherish the most? Why?

    C. "Praise is to faith what exercise is to the muscles of the body." If you wish to build faith, exercise it daily with praise. Do you agree or disagree? Explain. Can you overdo the praise exercise like you can physical exercise?

3. The author told how Satan tries to set her up for defeat before her speaking appointments. Recalling times the father of lies bombarded you with doubt and defeat, can you also see a pattern to his temptations? How will identifying such a pattern be an aid to your spiritual life?

4. Why does the preposition *in* make a difference in the verse, "Give thanks in all circumstances," instead of Give thanks *for* all circumstances? (see 1 Thessalonians 5:18).

A. Tell of a time when you claimed the promise in Psalm 23:4, "Though I walk through the valley of the shadow of death, I will fear no evil."

B. One of Old Testament Israel's most distasteful sins to God wasn't idolatry or adultery, but ingratitude. God hates ingratitude. Why do you think that is so?

C. "Giving thanks in all things gives us a 'God's eye view' of our world." Do you agree or disagree? Why?

More Than a Chorus Line

1. "Let us fix our eyes on Jesus." How does praising instead of complaining "fix our eyes on Jesus"?

2. Do you find the idea of indulging in *extravagant worship* uncomfortable? How does extravagant worship precede extravagant blessings?

A. The author mentioned examples of four extravagant worshipers—Abraham, Mary, Paul, and Silas. To which of these examples do you best relate? Which do you find disturbing? Explain.

B. How can worshiping God extravagantly defeat one's personal battle with insecurity? Which comes first? Extravagant worship or extravagant love? Explain.

3. "If I ask, the Holy Spirit will teach me how to worship." How does this circle of worship work?

Picking Up the Pieces

1. Picturing God as a loving Father is easy for those who grew up with loving fathers. It's far more difficult for the individual who suffered the ire of a bad father or the emptiness of an absent father. How is being a good parent evident in the way a parent shows his love?

A. Where do the similarities between earthly parenting and eternal parenting end? Explain.

B. "Wrestling is the only sport where the opponents never break contact." How would this be a comfort when you are "wrestling" with God over some issue in your life?

2. What was your reaction to Jim's murderous rampage in Vietnam? Are there sins so despicable that they shouldn't be forgiven? Explain.

A. What did the author mean when she wrote, "Forgiveness is all about Him, not about you"? Was Christ's sacrifice big enough to forgive your most grievous sin? Was His sacrifice big enough to forgive the sins of the 9/11 instigators?

B. Can God's children completely understand forgiveness? Is forgiveness unnatural to humanity? Explain.

C. Does true forgiveness take a generous dollop of divinity? If so how can we be accountable for our less-than-forgiving natures? Explain.

D. Do you believe God has forgiven your sins? Do you go deep-sea diving for them? Do you dig them up from the bottom of the ocean to inspect them a second or third time?

E. The author claims Philippians 3:13, 14, to defeat the memories of sins past. What do you do to put your past behind you? To move beyond your failures?

Practicing God's Presence

1. "You will fill me with joy in your presence." How does God's presence fill you with joy? Share a time when you experienced unmistakable joy in the presence of God.

2. "Music brings me into my Beloved's presence faster than any other medium." The author writes, "Praise choruses ... force me to my knees. There are hymns that cause me to fall prostrate at His feet."

A. Tell of a time when you experienced this type of extreme worship. What hymns or choruses have had a profound impact on your worship experience? Why?

B. Are you comfortable with the image of someone "falling down" to worship God? Why or why not? Can a person worship "too much"?

C. Why do you think shouting before God is foreign to western-ized worshipers? Is your worship style governed by Scripture or by your cultural heritage?

3. 1 Corinthians 13:12 reminds us that we see through a glass darkly. For just such a reason God placed within our minds the ability to visualize that which we cannot clearly see. We refer to this gift as imagination. When we ask, God will sanctify our imaginations so that we can grasp a clearer view of Him and of His love; He will open our eyes to truths that surpass human understanding. Perhaps that's what worship is all about—seeing as God sees.
   A. Are there limits to where we should allow the imagination to take us?
   B. What dangers can be found in an unleashed imagination? Should we restrict our thinking to only that which we can see, feel, taste, smell, and hear?
   C. "Every gift from God can be used for good and used for evil." True or false? Explain.

4. "It ain't over 'til it's over." How does the Yogi Berra quote apply to your spiritual journey?
   A. Read Philippians 1:6. What confidence does this promise give you in the Father's plan to save your loved ones?
   B. How does such a promise allow you to "ease up" on the preaching to your errant loved one and intensify the "loving"?
   C. Whose job is it to "convict" your precious loved one of sin? How should knowing this is true change your behavior toward others and toward yourself?

5. The author refers to anger, jealousy, and bitterness as "works of the flesh," hence high-ticketed luxuries a Christian cannot afford. Name some other "luxuries" that are too expensive for those who yearn to see the face of God.
   A. In Psalm 103, God promises to heal our diseases. References to God as our Healer can be found in many books of the Bible.

Explain how a child of God can come to Him with complete confidence and request divine healing.

    B. How do these high-ticketed items affect the way we come to God with our requests?

6. What was your reaction to the comment, "If Martha had sat down beside her sister, who would have fed everyone"? How would you have answered the question?

    A. When cash is short for the month and not turning in the tithe check could make all the difference, are you ever tempted to keep it back until the end of the month? Explain.

    B. How would such an action be a "Martha choice"?

    C. Martha wanted to please Jesus by serving Him her best. Yet she ended up accusing Him of not making Mary help her in the kitchen. What other emotions might have been involved in her actions?

7. "Living beautifully and loving it is not a fantasy. It's a choice." All the good things of life are choices.

    A. We may not be able to control all the bad that comes our way, but we can make choices to fill our lives with love, joy, peace, and hope by learning to stay in God's presence and to worship Him. Do you agree or disagree? Explain.

    B. "But you don't know what I'm going through." True, but God does—and He's only a breath away. Is such a statement too simple or too unrealistic?

    C. You can choose only for today, this hour, this moment. Yesterday is gone, and tomorrow doesn't belong to us. Share a text that supports this philosophy of living.

    D. If you completely live by this paradigm, what would change in your thinking? In your church? In your driving habits? In your interaction with those you love? With God?

If you enjoyed this book, you'll enjoy these as well:

A Time to Grow

Patricia R. Garey. A seasonal resource guide and nurturing program for women who want more for themselves and their families. This spiritual "almanac" includes daily devotional and Scripture readings, 52 vegetarian recipes, Sabbath craft and activity ideas, resource information and advice on marriage, parenting, and more.

0-8163-1961-8. Paperback.
US$14.99, Can$22.49.

Gardens of the Soul

Debbonnaire Kovacs. The care and nurture of your inner devotional life is the topic of this unique "gardening" guide. Drawing from her own background as a gardener, Debbonnaire uses a spiritual gardening allegory and her study of God's Word to teach us practical ways to cultivate a flourishing devotional life with God.

0-8163-1872-7. Paperback.
US$12.99, Can$19.49.

Devotional Retreats

Debbonnaire Kovacs. Draw closer to Jesus through devotional retreats—a method of using your five senses to study God's Word. Kovacs explains the purpose and joy of Christian meditation, and how it differs from the New Age counterfeit.

0-8163-1837-9. Paperback.
US$4.97, Can$7.47.

Order from your ABC by calling **1-800-765-6955**, or get online and shop our virtual store at **www.AdventistBookCenter.com**.
- •Read a chapter from your favorite book
- •Order online
- •Sign up for email notices on new products

Prices subject to change without notice.